Cleveland's Harbor

Cleveland's Harbor

The Cleveland–Cuyahoga County
Port Authority

by Jay C. Ehle

assisted by William D. Ellis
&
Nancy A. Schneider

THE KENT STATE UNIVERSITY PRESS
Kent, Ohio, & London, England

© 1996 by The Kent State University Press, Kent, Ohio 44242
All rights reserved
Library of Congress Catalog Card Number 95-33617
ISBN 0-87338-543-8
Manufactured in the United States of America

03 02 01 00 99 98 97 96   5 4 3 2 1

Library of Congress Cataloging-in-Publication Data
Ehle, Jay C. (Jay Clarence), 1917–
Cleveland's harbor: the Cleveland–Cuyahoga County Port Authority /
Jay C. Ehle with the assistance of William D. Ellis and Nancy A. Schneider.
p.   cm.
Includes index.
ISBN 0-87338-543-8 (alk. paper) ∞
1. Harbors—Ohio—Cleveland—History. 2. Cleveland–Cuyahoga County Port
Authority—History. I. Ellis, William Donahue. II. Schneider,
Nancy A., 1950–. III. Title.
HE554.C6E37   1996
386´.8´0977132—dc20   95-33617

British Library Cataloging-in-Publication data are available.

To the hundreds of people who made the Port,
and to the thousands who made it their port of call.

Contents

Preface

I did not volunteer to write this book. Port Chairman Sterling Glover and several public officials shanghaied me into writing this history, feeling that I had the closest and longest association with the Port from the Board viewpoint.

Since the real story began long before there was a Board, I chose not to disturb the historic narrative with first-person remarks.

As I got deeper into the work, I began to realize how much the story needs telling for the benefit of the citizens of all port cities.

Few know the conflicting pressures on seaports. On the one hand, the leadership, official and volunteer, looks to the ports for economic advance, especially jobs. On the other hand, the same leadership presses in on the Port's space with well-meant civic projects for tourism and entertainment.

Most leaders realize that ports compete with other ports, but they forget that ports also compete with other modes of transportation. Rising rent and lockage fees drive many cargoes to the railroads. Ports are expected to make foreign vessels welcome, yet their first greeting is by the expressionless face of big government, U.S. Customs and Immigration.

Great Lakes cities look to their ports to foster exports, yet our government requires that 40 percent of government exports—wheat, arms—ride in American hulls, even though practically no U.S. ocean ships serve the Great Lakes.

Bracing against this weather, somewhat heroic port staffs work to make it work.

And for me, personally, well, there's something about ships . . .

Jay C. Ehle

Acknowledgments

I gratefully acknowledge the main body of Great Lakes literature, including the notes of the early surveyors of the Connecticut Western Reserve, that I used in writing this book.

I am also grateful for the help of my maritime colleagues who gave me their time for interviews; the help of John Hubbell, director of the Kent State University Press; and the assistance of William D. Ellis, Nancy A. Schneider, and Marcia Siedel of Editorial, Inc., who are also the editors of *Inland Seas,* the quarterly journal of the Great Lakes Historical Society.

Foreword

by A. F. Fugaro

There is no simple definition of what a port authority is. Across the country the organizations and purposes of port authorities vary from community to community. Some states, Maryland, Georgia, and Indiana, for example, have a statewide port authority. In New York Harbor, a bistate port authority operates the marine and air terminals within the area. On the other end of the spectrum, Washington State has over eighty port authorities within its limits.

In Ohio, all port authorities are created under a specific section of the Ohio Revised Code, yet no two of these authorities function in the same manner. Essentially, a port authority is a creation of the community and is what the community wants it to be.

At its inception, the Cleveland–Cuyahoga County Port Authority was looked on as a vehicle to achieve effective, professional management of lakefront maritime operations. As this account chronicles, the community expectations and the use of the port authority powers have evolved over the years.

With six directors appointed by the City of Cleveland and three by the county commissioners, the make-up of the Port's Board of Directors changes slightly each year as members are replaced. This evolving membership means that the emphasis, policies, or objectives of the Port Authority at any one point in time may also be subject to change.

As this history will show, the individuals appointed as directors have come from a wide variety of backgrounds. Business leaders, labor leaders, attorneys, developers, religious leaders, community leaders, and shipping executives, among others, have all been appointed to the Port Authority. This variety has brought a wealth of insight and expertise to the deliberations and decisions of the Board. How well the community has benefited from this resource will be left to the judgment of the reader.

The year 1993 marked the twenty-fifth anniversary of the Cleveland Port Authority. As the second quarter-century of existence has commenced, a more mature Authority with broader community perspectives has evolved. Nowhere is this more evident than in the economic development activities undertaken by the Port Authority in recent years. The expanded use of foreign trade zones and the increasing involvement in lakefront development are examples of the changing role of the Port Authority.

As this is being written, the Greater Cleveland area is seeing major projects come into being. Gateway Development saw its primary element, Jacobs Field and the adjacent Gund Arena, successfully inaugurated, and both are welcoming large crowds. On the lakefront, the international Rock and Roll Hall of Fame and Museum opened under the aegis of the Port Authority. Yesterday's dreams are becoming today's realities.

"Change" and "progress" are clearly the words to describe the ambience of Cleveland. The Cleveland–Cuyahoga County Port Authority will undoubtedly play an increasingly important role as the lakefront and downtown areas move ahead. However, in order to progress, it is necessary to know where we are, how we got there, and where we want to go. This history is both timely and essential as the Port Authority plans for an exciting future.

Cleveland's Harbor

1

Frontier Port

Captain Ramagathan of the Indian vessel *Punica,* outbound from the Seaway with 18,000 tons of coiled steel from LTV for Taiwan, received a call from the new master of the incoming *Federal Maas* bringing 12,000 tons of wire rod and structural steel from Antwerp to Cleveland. The acting master of the *Maas* wanted a *captain's* opinion of Cleveland's port.

The answer from Ramagathan crackled through in that extra-British accent of India: "Easy to come into. Generally without tugs. You get accurate departure times. Good crew port. Close to town for shopping. Every kind of ethnic restaurant. Good trip to you, Captain."

The *Maas* headed for the mouth of the St. Lawrence, which would take her to the center of North America. This ship, under several masters, over many years and voyages, had been joining the economies of the two continents at Cleveland.

Since before Marco Polo, the waters have been the main roads to link populations. And water invented Cleveland. It became her front door and her back door. It fed her. It determined her character, vocations, and international role.

The importance of the front door, Lake Erie, was to give Cleveland a northwest reach all the way to iron-bearing Minnesota and northeast all the way to Europe via the Erie Canal and later the St. Lawrence.

The importance of the south-facing back door was predicted by the long-sighted former surveyor, G. Washington, who wrote on October 10, 1784, to Benjamin Harrison, governor of Virginia, "It has always been my opinion that the shortest and least expensive communication with the *invaluable back country* would be [to] let the courses and distances be taken to the mouth of the Muskingum and up that river to the carrying place to the Cuyahoga, down the Cuyahoga to Lake Erie."

Despite civically inspired works crediting General Moses Cleaveland with envisioning a great future port, none of these advantages could have been apparent to him as his crew poled a small boat through the marsh grass a dozen years later looking for the mouth of the Cuyahoga River.

The development of a port at this river mouth was then unlikely. No encircling peninsular arms reached out from the escarpment in 1796 to block the northwest winds and enclose a calm harbor where a vessel could ease up to a protected mooring.

A captain with any draft could not shelter in the early Cuyahoga River mouth, even if he could find it. The meandering river paralleled the lake shore in a marsh, finally entering the lake over a broad swamplike delta.

The most far-sighted of men could not predict the steel industry that would someday be the main business of the port; nor could they predict its international scope. The iron ore

was not here, nor was the coking coal or the limestone.

The Port of Cleveland was made less by nature than by a relay of remarkable men.

General Cleaveland's Port

Despite the obscure mouth of the Cuyahoga River, General Moses Cleaveland forced it to become a port of entry in 1796. The chunky, dark-skinned general had a commission from the Connecticut Land Company to survey its three million acres of New Connecticut. (The company had purchased Connecticut's Western Reserve in the Ohio Country for about 40 cents per acre.) He was charged with measuring it and surveying it into townships five miles square so that the absentee owners in Connecticut could resell their lands (ultimately 216 townships).

En route to the Cuyahoga, the general split his surveyor force of fifty-two people into four teams. The larger force came overland from Conneaut to work west along the Reserve's south line, the forty-first parallel, marking off the ranges. The general led a small headquarters group in boats from Buffalo.

He had a one-season target and a budget of $7,000. He had already lost one of his five boats in a storm; and he had lost $2,500 in Buffalo because the Mohawks and Senecas (Red Jacket and Chief Joseph Brant [Thayenanege]) of the Six Nations would not let his men pass on to the Reserve.

Arrogant, vulgar, and imperious when he could be, humble and gracious when he had to be, Cleaveland's strength was negotiation. He negotiated genially and shrewdly, but so did Chief Brant. The cost of the negotiation was $500 immediate cash plus $2,000 in goods and cash later. But the greater cost was five days' delay. That plus a previous delay by the British at Oswego made him very late in getting the survey completed and his crew home to Connecticut before ice closed the lake.

On July 22, 1796, he raised the mouth of the Cuyahoga. The party sculled inland through reeds until they came to a solid ledge under the towering east bank.

Cleaveland made use of the Cuyahoga two ways. Its hundred-mile length was in a huge U shape, which gave him navigable supply communication by canoe to his survey teams working the pathless hardwood forest. And later, immigrating purchasers of the company's lands could use the U-shaped river to get close to their property.

He selected the east bank for his survey headquarters and for the region's main town because legally (1795 treaty of Greenville) the Cuyahoga was the western boundary of the United States. West of it was Indian. He knew that ultimately he would be forced to trespass in order to complete measurement of the Reserve, but he would not irritate the Senecas earlier than necessary.

Though the full survey story is fascinating, the relevant point here is that General Cleaveland first made the Cuyahoga's mouth the northern port of entry to the Ohio frontier.

On October 12, in a snowstorm, Cleaveland's diminished, sick, and disgruntled party "left Cuyahoga at three o'clock 17 minutes for HOME" (surveyor Holley's journal). The general received a cold reception at home in Connecticut, having overspent without completing the survey. Additionally, he had committed the company to give free lots to two men he left on the Reserve to guard supplies. The company would need to assess members for a second survey crew.

The general would not return to Ohio.

Lorenzo Carter's Port

The second survey party came earlier the next year, and included the Reverend Seth Hart as surveyor and Seth Pease as astronomer and chief surveyor. While they were finishing the survey of Cleaveland (township 7, range 12) in May, there arrived among them a tall, scarce-of-fat stranger from Connecticut via Canada. Lorenzo Carter brought resolve. He also brought a wife, a son, and a household girl, Chloe Inches. Chloe met and fell in love with Canadian Mr. Clement, and Reverend Hart officiated at their wedding—the first to be performed in Cleaveland.

While the surveyors had built small, temporary huts, the hard-muscled Carter, with the ice-blue eyes, built a large, permanent-looking house. When it was finished, he built another beside it. And when that one was completed, he built a connecting structure between. Unlike the transient-minded surveyors, Carter took a proprietary attitude about the place, and when the second survey crew fled east in October 1797, Carter was the leading man in the nearly empty village.

The Connecticut Land Company gave some free lots to a handful of surveyors to stay and guard the investment, leaving a total of only seven families behind, but Carter acted as if the seven were the cadre for a city of hundreds. He built a boat to ferry the possible on-coming throngs across the river. He cultivated the Indians as long-term neighbors. He opened his house as an inn for travelers, urging them to settle here. He lent his house for those two necessities of a real town—church and tavern. To supply the latter, he built a still.

In 1799 the Cuyahoga River threatened to wipe out Cleaveland. After the spring floods, the delta at the mouth backed up the slow flowing river with stagnating water that, at midsummer, bred clouds of mosquitoes. The population was so sickened by malaria that they could barely crawl to feed themselves. Lorenzo Carter, with the assistance of his son and his good Indian neighbor, Seneca, fed the entire community. When the fever lifted, several families moved away.

The village was also nearly wiped out by the absentee company trustees' ignorance over their high asking prices. Company agent Turhand Kirtland wrote to General Cleaveland explaining that Carter and two other families were the only *real* settlers. He explained that Major Carter had been the most useful citizen and had helped keep other settlers here, "for which he never received even the thanks of the company." [The company had refused his offer of hard money for thirty acres]; ". . . and he is determined to remove to some other part . . . unless he can obtain better terms than I am authorized to give."

People continued leaving the region despite Carter's establishment of a ferry, inn, tavern, church, and school. Deciding that the few settlers upstream needed to get their surplus goods to a market, Carter, with the help of some settlers, built a boat, the thirty-ton *Zephyr*. With a team of eight work cattle, they hauled it down the riverbank into the water. The flat-bottomed boat was a poor sailor, but she was able to stay afloat and carry small cargo. Murray and Bixby, next built a sixty-ton ship.

As scholars look back on this settlement, they increasingly see Carter as the man who held the port.

Levi Johnson's Port

In 1809 a young carpenter from New York State walked over the Lake Erie ice to Cleaveland. Levi Johnson had been working with wood since age fourteen. His skill was such that the Cleaveland people put him to work immediately building large structures—houses, barns, sawmills, and a warehouse to service Lorenzo Carter's *Zephyr*. He became Cleaveland's largest builder.

During the war scare in 1812, someone told Johnson of a beached and damaged boat at the mouth of the Rocky River. He took some of his builder team there, repaired the boat, and sailed it back to Cleaveland, where he thoroughly rebuilt it.

When the Battle of Lake Erie ended, Levi bought all the potatoes he could find in town and sailed them to Put-in-Bay and sold them to Perry's fleet for a dollar a bushel. The army put Levi's small boat to work carrying cargo to garrisons in Detroit.

Levi saw the possibilities. He built a larger boat, the *Pilot* (estimated thirty-five-ton displacement). Twenty-eight yoke of oxen pulled her, on roll-

ers, to the Cuyahoga. As soon as the *Pilot* was afloat, she was hired to haul troops and munitions from Buffalo to Detroit in 1814. Business was so good that Johnson built another, *Lady's Master*. And his shipping business grew. In need of a building in which to store merchandise awaiting shipment or claim by consignees of imports, he built a warehouse near the mouth of the Cuyahoga.

Business went so well that Levi planned a third vessel. Since his boats were becoming progressively larger, it was getting increasingly difficult to move them from his cabin to the river. Therefore, he built a small shipyard on the river at the foot of Eagle Street. He laid the keel of his *Neptune* in 1815 and launched her in the spring of 1816. This vessel, too, was quickly earning money. In 1817 the *Neptune*'s cargo, bound for Michilimackinac, Michigan, included oxen, calves, sheep, whiskey, pork, flour, butter, tallow, and grindstones.

On September 1, 1818, the stunned villagers gathered at the waterfront. Anchored offshore was the most amazing sight—the *Walk-in-the-Water*, the first steam vessel to sail Lake Erie and the upper Lakes.

The mouth of the Cuyahoga had become a port of call. However, it was still a hostile marsh on a long west loop of the river. Men had long wanted to open a new mouth to the east in order to make the river a straight channel to open water.

As late as 1822, Johnson's *Mercator*, drawing only thirty-nine inches, could not enter the silted river mouth. The U.S. Congress authorized $5,000 to build a pier six hundred feet into the lake from the west bank, but the sandbar re-formed as fast as it was excavated. A matching pier was built on the east bank, but ice and northwest storms blew it out.

The problem continued until 1827 when engineers invented an efficient plan to harness the river's own strength. Before the spring floods, they dammed off the last leg of the river at the curve where it turned abruptly west. When the flood waters rose and could not turn west, they flushed out a straight-ahead channel in the land, creating a new mouth straight to open water.

Levi Johnson had seen the steamer *Walk-in-the-Water*. He began to study that vessel and the steamer *Ontario* on Lake Ontario. Then in league with the Turhooven brothers, he began construction of a steam vessel, the *Enterprise*. They built it just east of the river on the lake front. The sixty-horsepower engine and its machinery were hauled from Pittsburgh by oxen.

The *Enterprise* was designed with fine passenger space in addition to cargo. Built in eighteen months, the vessel was a commercial success right from her christening on May 10, 1826.

Cleveland was the home port to a steam vessel, a significant step.

Alfred Kelley's Port

Following the War of 1812, the Ohio frontier slid into a depression that deepened into the 1820s. Good Eastern dollars would not flow west as the frontiersman had no economical way to ship revenue-producing products or farm produce east. If a settler shipped grain overland, it cost him $5.00 per hundred weight per hundred miles, making his grain uncompetitive in the East.

The settlers had to trade in currencies issued by local banks. Typically a local dollar lost value at a penny a mile as it moved away from its issuing bank. Settlers could not meet their land payment installments. Sheriffs' hammers fell on Ohio.

A precocious and prickly Cleveland attorney, Alfred Kelley, the youngest Ohio legislator, was impressed with Governor Ethan Allen Brown's longtime push for a canal connecting Lake Erie to the Ohio River. Any farmer near such a canal could economically ship produce to Lake Erie, thence to Buffalo, across New York's Erie Canal to the Hudson and down the Hudson to the New York City market, or south on the canal to the Ohio River and down the Mississippi to the Gulf of Mexico and the world.

The bachelor governor was married to the canal bill he had been pushing in the legislature for six years. Kelley joined the push. Like Brown, he was not afraid of big numbers. But it was not hard for the anti-canal legislators to laugh the canal bill off the capitol floor. There was only $133,000 in the state treasury, and Brown and Kelley were talking a cost of five million dollars!

Governor Brown left the governorship for the U.S. Senate. Kelley inherited the leadership of the fight, battling turnpike and stagecoach interests and legislators from districts remote from the proposed canal. It also meant fighting for the route he believed best, with the northern terminal at Cleveland, though Sandusky, Milan, and Toledo had very strong claims. Opponents charged him with conflict of interest, with favoring his own town.

Kelley and colleagues made political trades to get the canal bill passed and then courageously pursued the enormous funding challenge while huge Trumbull County announced it would withhold tax money.

Kelley and Micajah Williams, the two leading canal commissioners during construction, battled weather, labor, scheming contractors, malaria, and legislators determined to stop the construction. Twice, the exposure and the work nearly killed Kelley, whose health, despite his youth, became fragile.

However, the northern leg of the canal, from Akron to Cleveland, opened on July 4, 1827. For the open-ing, a ceremonial canal boat, the *State of Ohio,* traveled the thirty-eight miles from Akron to Cleveland accompanied by band music and cannon salutes and carrying the governor and dignitaries who waved to crowds on the banks. The more important event, however, occurred an hour later, when, after the dignitaries had all gone to a state dinner, an unnamed canal boat traveled from Akron without music, banners, and distinguished guests but *with* a cargo of flour and whiskey.

Economic improvements usually crawl forward. This one was revolutionary . . . an economic miracle.

Wheat from Ohio's interior, which would hardly move down state for 25 cents a bushel, found a market at the mouth of the Cuyahoga at 75 cents.

The canal cut into the Cuyahoga near its mouth, where canal cargo from the back country transferred to outbound schooners or into commission agent warehouses for resale. Thus, one riverbank near the mouth became a forest of schooner masts, while the other was lined with canal boats, mule barns, warehouses, and commission agent offices, one of which would much later be staffed by a serious young bookkeeper named John D. Rockefeller.

Out of the frontier interior floated canal-borne grain, lumber, salt, and coal to the Port of Cleveland for transshipment east. That traffic returned good Eastern dollars with which Westerners could pay for what they could not yet manufacture in the forest.

Hence, into the frontier interior by canal now flowed Eastern manufactured products of brass, glass, and iron via the busy Port of Cleveland. Also floating into the interior was some of life's romance—dress shoes and silk, mirrors, and combs—signs of good times.

2

The Early Shipbuilders

In the cold months for two decades after the canal opening, a blinding sight on the Cuyahoga was the dawn lighting up the ice-glazed maze of riggings. Eighty or ninety schooners could be tied up there—schooners from Buffalo, Detroit, Conneaut, Erie, Lorain, and even Manitowoc.

In the late 1830s and 1840s, the ports of Vermilion and Huron led Cleveland in shipbuilding. Ashtabula and Sandusky were also building ships. When the Ohio Canal opened, Vermilion had already launched seven schooners. In Milan, Ben Abbott laid keel for the *Mary Abbott,* beginning Milan's career as a shipbuilder. He eventually broke champagne (or hard cider) against the bows of seventy-five schooners.

This furnished work for a lot of men. One of the most dramatic was John Malvin.

Malvin, with healed whip marks on his back, arrived with his wife in Cleveland by canal in April 1829. They were en route to Canada. His wife, however, became depressed at going so far from her aging father who was enslaved in Kentucky. Malvin, therefore, agreed to give up Canada and seek carpenter work in Cleveland. In his autobiography, *North Into Freedom,* Malvin explained, "But my color was an obstacle. I managed, however, to obtain employment as a cook on the schooner *Aurora* that sailed . . . between Mackinaw and Buffalo."

It turned out that one of the owners of the *Aurora,* J. H. Hudson, had bought a steam mill from Leonard

Case, Sr., and P. B. Andrews. He wanted Malvin to run this steam plant even though Malvin knew nothing about it. Malvin recognized the opportunity and guarded it carefully. At night he disassembled the engine, laying each piece in sequence so that he could reassemble it exactly. He became an expert on that engine.

Malvin valued that job, because behind him was a hard odyssey.

John Malvin was authorized to preach among the slaves and make marriages among them, though he was unlicensed as a Baptist preacher in Virginia because it was illegal to license a black man.

He had gained his own freedom by the death of an owner. And in 1827, at age thirty-two, he took leave of his parents. With only an extra shirt and his "freedom paper," he walked north on the Winchester Road three hundred miles. He started across the Ohio River toward Marietta as a passenger in a rowboat. Seeing the black passenger, a fugitive slave hunter on the south bank ordered the boat to turn back. Malvin presented his freedom papers and was allowed to cross to Marietta. After reaching Marietta and before going to Cleveland, he spent two hard years along the banks of the Ohio River, where the harsh Black Code Laws were in force.

With that behind him, he began the steam plant job for Mr. Hudson. Respect developed between the two men to the point where Malvin even revealed to Hud-son his plan to buy the freedom of his father-in-law, Caleb Dorsey. He could do this for $100 down and $300 in two payments over two years. With Hudson's encouragement, Malvin circulated a subscription paper, raising the $100 that, when received in Kentucky, released the old man and brought him to Cleveland.

Near Hudson's Mill on Academy Lane was a small brick building owned by a Mr. Brewster, who allowed the First Baptist congregation to meet there. While in Cincinnati, Malvin had been licensed to preach. He preached in this building on Academy Lane and in Rockport and Euclid and other villages.

The pressure to pay the two notes for his father-in-law's freedom required extra income. Malvin was able to buy on easy terms from Abraham Wright a vessel named the *Grampus*. However, he was refused a license to sail by the deputy collector on grounds of color. The chief collector, Samuel Starkweather, overheard this. Starkweather, future mayor of Cleveland, ruled that if Malvin had a right to drive a horse and wagon he had a right to sail a boat.

With license in hand, Malvin got a contract to haul limestone and cedar posts from Kelleys Island to Cleveland. He became the first black vessel owner to use the Port.

Malvin later sold his boat and in 1839 sailed as a deckhand on the steamer *Rochester* (Buffalo–Chicago).

The following year he bought a canal boat from S. R. Hutchinson & Company. He put his boat, the *Auburn*, to work hauling wheat and passengers from the interior to Cleveland. His crew was one white steersman, one black steersman, two white drivers, one black bowman, and one black female cook.

While working as captain of the *Auburn*, Malvin launched a historic program. In about 1832 he called a meeting of black men to organize a school for black children, who were excluded from schools. John Hudson let them hold school in the mill. "We hired a half breed to teach . . . paying him $20 a month." He taught for three months; then Clarissa Wright taught for two and a half months; and then M. M. Clark, from the East, taught for three months.

In Columbus in 1835, Malvin called a statewide convention of black men to organize the School Fund Society to establish schools for black children in various towns. The convention established a second school in Cleveland, one in Springfield, and one in Cincinnati, where a citizen gave them twenty-five acres.

Over the years, Malvin's life attracted to the black community the support of some strong white leaders who became an informal advisory group. Among them were R. F. Payne, Edwin Cowles, M. C. Younglove, and John Huntington.

Especially supportive was the Reverend Aiken, who, when the Ohio Fugitive Slave Law passed, called a meeting at his First Presbyterian Church and denounced the law. It was resolved at that meeting that if any fugitive slave were arrested in Cleveland, all church bells should ring as notice to the people to assemble. Younglove put up a five-dollar reward for the first church sexton to ring a church bell on each such occasion.

Malvin arranged several conventions of black leaders in Ohio. When the Civil War broke out, Malvin called a meeting of all Cleveland blacks at National Hall on Public Square. From the meeting came a determination to send a delegation to the governor to request permission to raise a black militia company. The state politely declined; but the fact that Malvin's people could even make such an approach shows how far they had come since 1830.

At age eighty-three, Malvin wrote, "I thank God for letting me live long enough to witness the change wrought in the condition of colored people. It seems . . . a miracle . . . . I firmly believe it to be the interposition of Divine Providence." He died two years later, on September 29, 1880, and was buried in Erie

Cemetery. The *Cleveland Leader* printed a full column headed, "Eventful Career and Noble Work of a Worthy Man Whose Thoughts Were of His People."

DECEASED

John Malvin, a black native of Virginia (city unknown) resided at 391 Sterling Avenue in Cleveland, Ohio. He was married, however, his wife's name is unknown.

He died at the age of 85, on July 31, 1880, from dropsy. His physician was J. C. Sanders.

He was buried August 1, 1880, at Erie Cemetery located on 9th Street off Carnegie Avenue.

He is buried in Section 3, Lot 67, Tier N½, Grave 1S. This was the 3rd grave of a three (3) grave lot Mr. Malvin owned.

Eliza Hall, 33 years old, was buried October 21, 1842, in the first grave, and Fannie Dorsey, who died from old age (85 years old), was buried November 9, 1862, in the second.

Malvin's work had brought the black man a long way forward from the arrival of the first black man in Cleveland, known only as Ben. While Ben had a severely lame foot from frostbite, he felt he could get around enough to do useful work for somebody. Any amount of pay would be all right since he had worked all his life only for food and shelter on the Young plantation in Kentucky country.

Major Carter took him in for the same pay rate.

In 1806 a smooth professional slave catcher caught up with Ben and talked him into returning to the Young farm in Kentucky. He put Ben on his horse while the horse walked down the old Carter Road heading for Kentucky. We don't know whether Carter told some settlers about Ben's decision or not. But suddenly two armed men leapt out of the woods and yelled, "Ben you damned fool! Jump off that horse and head into the woods!"

Ben jumped, crab legging into the woods.

The Kentuckian did not pursue. However, Ben could not know that. He became invisible.

However, that winter the son of Major Spafford and a younger brother of Nathan Perry were out hunting in the West Bank wilderness and became lost. Wandering for some hours, they came upon some horse tracks. They followed these to a small, hidden hut. There was one person living there.

It was Ben, the first black resident of what became Cuyahoga County.

In 1831 John Nicholson and son opened a repair yard, Cleveland Dry Dock Company, and advertised haul out or docking entrance fees in the *Cleveland Herald:*

Schooners exceeding 26-ton, $10.00
Every day after seven days, $2.00
Schooners under 25 tons, $5.00
Every day after seven days, $1.00
Scows $2.00, after three days, 50c/day

In 1835, Seth W. Johnson opened a repair yard that quickly became a shipbuilding yard. In August he completed and launched the 368-ton side-wheeler *Robert Fulton.* Johnson teamed with E. Tisdale and built a marine railway and floating dock in their yard in Ohio City (west bank). The *Constellation* was one of the yard's best-known vessels.

In 1841 Captain George W. Jones moved his shipbuilding business from Lorain's Black River to Cleveland. To escape a farming career in Lorain he paid a traveling draftsman all his boyhood savings plus a pair of boots to teach him the science of drafting vessels. Thus began a distinguished career in shipbuilding, first in Lorain and then in Cleveland. He invented the arch for the wooden freighters and is credited as designer of the iron-hulled *Onoko,* a preview of the evolving bulk carrier design.

In 1843 Captain Jones built the *Emigrant,* the first propeller-driven ship to be launched in the Cuyahoga; this came just two years after the launching of the famous *Vandalia* of New York, the first propeller ship on the Great Lakes and the first *commercial* propeller-driven ship in the

world. The *Emigrant,* pushed by two-cylinder engines from Cuyahoga Steam Furnace, carried fifty-five passengers regularly. Jones would frequently employ eighty men.

In 1846 Cleveland yards launched one steamer, six propellers, and fourteen schooners; and in 1847 production increased to twenty-seven schooners, four scows, two steamers, and three propellers—$440,000 worth of vessels. The major builders were De Grote and Levayes, Sanford and Moses, and S. A. Turner.

The banks of the Cuyahoga in the 1840s became the leading shipbuilding port on the Great Lakes. Sadly, much of the demand was caused by a terrible attrition rate of groundings, sinkings, and boiler explosions.

Thomas Quayle came from the Isle of Man in 1811. He finished his apprenticeship in Cleveland and started his own yard in 1847 with James Cody, and they were later joined by Luther Moses. They sometimes had seven hulls on the stocks at once, and one year built thirteen boats. Quayle & Sons established a quality reputation for Cleveland vessels. When Thomas Quayle retired from the company in 1882, his sons continued building as long as wooden shipbuilding survived in Cleveland.

Captain Eli Peck's yard built many vessels, including the 200-ton *Jenny Lind.* Much later in this chronicle we will meet Peck again when he builds a vessel that will revolutionize Great Lakes ship design.

One of the most famous Cleveland-built ships was Captain Jones's 260-foot passenger steamer *Empire*. Completed in 1844 at 1,136 tons, she was 200 tons larger than any steamer in the world. She was the first vessel to be launched sideways, which later became standard.

Just before the Civil War, a small out-of-town shipbuilder quietly took a small office in Cleveland, where many orders for cargo were placed. He had no yard in town, so some shippers were surprised at how much capacity he could offer.

When Alva Bradley was walking behind a plow horse at age ten on his father's farm in Brownhelm, Ohio, he already knew this was not the best view of life. He found work as a tamper in the charcoal phase of an iron works near Vermilion. He burned his leg there, incurring pain that would follow him sixty years.

Bradley loved to watch the schooners scudding along shore. He applied for work as a sailor on a vessel; however, underage, he was instead accepted as the cook's assistant. But that was the chance he needed. He advanced up ranks rapidly to captain, hauling lumber and wheat to Canada.

At age twenty-six and single, he found two partners and contracted for a ship to be built at Vermilion, the 104-ton *South America*. Having rounded up a cargo, Bradley sailed his own vessel to profit. That was a first step in building the Bradley Fleet. As a young vessel master sailing frequently to Detroit, Bradley became acquainted with the Edisons, who named their son Thomas Alva Edison.

Two years before the Civil War erupted, Bradley moved his headquarters to Cleveland, which at that time dominated the buying of shipping. A few years later, he began building his ships in Cleveland.

What Kinds of Ships?

In the decades from 1830 to 1850, captains and builders learned that fore-and-aft was better than square rigging for the Great Lakes. On the oceans a master would set his sails and leave them alone for hours, even days. But in close lake waters vessels had to change course quickly, often upwind. Hence, lake builders went to brigantines or barkentines with square sails only on the foremast. Generally the trade called them schooners. Some were schooner barges, shallow draft and boxy, and some had retractable center boards for shallow ports.

Ships that wanted to go through the Welland Canal were limited to 140 feet and were shallow, flat bottomed, and boxy. The bowsprits slanted up sharply to miss lock gates. Timber hookers carried a couple horses to winch lumber aboard and hoist sails.

Some of these schooners were very fast, making twenty miles per hour and even sailing outside the Great Lakes. For example, in 1849 the barkentine *Eureka* sailed from Cleveland for California, and as early as 1847 the schooner *New Brunswick* sailed 18,000 bushels of wheat from Chicago directly to Liverpool, England.

By 1838 the combined value of Cleveland imports and exports was $20 million. Arrivals at Cleveland Harbor that year included 1,095 sail and 1,318 steam vessels.

Cargoes?

Westbound vessels brought immigrants from Buffalo to homestead in Illinois and the western frontier. Soon thereafter the homesteaders' wheat began flowing east *to* Buffalo. Whiskey, grain, and corn out of the Ohio interior floated up the Ohio and Erie Canal and then sailed by schooner to Michigan. Manufactured products of all kinds flowed from the East to Cleveland and then by canal into the interior.

The railroad-building era at first threatened shipbuilders with the notion that the public would feel safer on rails in view of the terrible record of sinkings on the Great Lakes. Railroaders soon discovered, however, that rights of way and rail construction built mountains of cost, while the "rails" across Lake Erie were free. And while locomotive builders were making trains go faster and faster, they were less skilled at stopping them: train wrecks were rivaling vessel sinkings and explosions.

Shipbuilders will enter the story later when the Lake commerce takes a pronounced shift in character created by a handful of Cleveland men who were fascinated by exciting rumors coming down the Lakes from upper Michigan.

3

Cleveland Men Look North

All of this shipping experience would profoundly mold the character of the city and its harbor because of some very specific events so far northwest that Henry Clay called them "beyond the moon."

In the 1840s demand for brass was rising. Men in Cleveland were interested in finding the copper and zinc needed for brass making. Reports had been drifting down the Lakes to Cleveland about wonderful caches of copper up north on the shores of Lake Superior, lumps as big as pumpkins. Cleveland men were ready to put up the large dollars needed to make brass, but they needed to know for certain if the copper was really there. In 1845 they hired a Dr. Lang Cassels to explore the upper Mississippi in order to confirm this and then again in 1846 to explore Michigan's Upper Peninsula.

Cassels had come to Cleveland in 1843 at age thirty-five to head the Western Reserve Medical School, bringing with him a wonderful new tool, a microscope. Beyond medicine, Dr. Cassels was one of those early polymathic scientists; he was interested in chemistry, botany, and mineralogy. His credentials for this place and this time were towering. He made these explorations for several groups of businessmen. His adventures in the Indian country of Michigan's Upper Peninsula were dramatic, and he met other explorers there who were acting for other business groups.

When Dr. Cassels returned to Cleveland, he was asked to lecture publicly about the northern lands. His audiences were fascinated by his display of copper and silver. But one group was especially interested in handfuls of a red-and-gray dirt.

When he was on his way home from the Upper Peninsula, Cassels met A. V. Berry, another explorer from a group called the Jackson Company. Berry was hauling 300 pounds of ore samples he had taken from a mile-long mountain that Chief Marji-Gesick's Indians revered because lightning played around it on hot nights. Berry was impressed with Cassels, and Cassels was impressed with the red-and-gray ore samples. They exchanged information about their missions. Berry then said that if the men paying Cassels would share the expenses of holding the land claims and building a road into the claim, he would direct Cassels to the source of the red earth.

Cassels apparently felt empowered to make that commitment. He borrowed Berry's boat and rowed back along the south shore of Lake Superior to the Carp River. Two miles beyond that he found the mountain (later called Cleveland Mountain). A thousand feet wide at its base, it rose nearly straight, 180 feet, above a small stream. After scraping away a thin skin of moss on a vertical face, Cassels was staring at fantastically interwoven veins of brilliantly colored red-and-steel-gray earth. He traced these bands for the mile-long length of the mountains.

Cassels obtained a claim paper on this mountain and returned to Cleveland.

Many attending his public lectures were unconvinced of commercial feasibility. However, several Cleveland businessmen were forming into companies to exploit the ores of the north. One of these men was W. A. Adair. He went up to the iron range to see for himself and to help hold the land claim Cassels had made. In the midst of land claim wars, companies were burning down each other's marks and log cabins and shooting at each other's representatives.

When Adair returned, he and ten friends assembled in April 1847 and agreed to form a company to buy Marji-Gesick's mountain as soon as the government permitted purchases.

On November 9 the eleven shareholders formally organized as Cleveland Iron Mining Company. Later, four others were admitted, including John Outhwaite, who became the largest shareholder. The third largest was a young attorney recently arrived in Cleveland, Samuel Livingston Mather, a descendant of Cotton Mather. The first stock certificate was handwritten on a sheet of notebook paper.

Two other companies, Marquette and Jackson, planning to mine ore up on Superior, inland of Marquette, actually built smelting furnaces there. The Cleveland Iron Company planned to do the same. They planned the whole process down to and including a net annual profit of $24,000. But these plans were made in warm Cleveland offices, not up north on the steep side of a freezing mountain where food had to come from 700 miles away and only Indians stayed for the winter.

After some conflicts with the other companies on the range, Cleveland Iron secured title to 640 acres of the mountain. Not until 1850 would the federal government sell the land. In December 1851, when the Michigan legislature approved their incorporation in that state, the Cleveland men met in Samuel Mather's Cleveland law office; there they adopted bylaws and elected Dr. Isaac L. Hewitt president. Hewitt was a friend of Cassels.

George E. Freeman, who had gone out to look at the property in 1848 and prophesied staggering problems of making iron in the north woods, resigned as trustee. He assigned his shares to Hewitt and Outhwaite. His resignation was meaningful. He had seen firsthand that the Marquette and Jackson mining companies were going broke. Men hated working the charcoal kilns and would not stay during the harsh winters. Sometimes winds across the Upper Peninsula blew out the fire of the charcoal pits. And one payday Czar Jones of the

Jackson Company could not make payroll. The workmen openly discussed suspending him midair by the neck. Jones hired Peter White as a guide to lead him out of the wilderness. At sunset he fled.

This was the condition of the iron business on Lake Superior at midcentury.

But in the Cleveland Iron Company there was an iron man, Samuel Mather. As grim as the prospects looked, the Cleveland Iron Company gathered its strength to buy the struggling Marquette Company. Before that plan was finalized, however, the Marquette Company made one move that changed the industry and the Great Lakes commerce profoundly.

Marquette's way of operating had been to chop out the ore in the summer when the ground was soft. Since the weight of the ore mired the cart wheels into the earth, they waited for the freeze to sled the ore down off the mountain to the smelter. Then they shipped finished pig iron (pig-shaped iron blooms) down the Great Lakes for sale, usually at a loss. In addition to the hardships of mining and smelting in the cold north loomed the arduous shipping around the twenty-foot drop in the turbulent waters beginning at Sault Ste. Marie. The iron pigs had to be unloaded upstream of the Sault, portaged around it laboriously and expensively, and reloaded below on another vessel for the trip down the Lakes.

A Cargo Change

On July 7, 1852, however, the Marquette Company shipped six barrels of raw iron ore downstream to Cleveland to be smelted into iron there instead of in the north.

That was a prophetic shift. Shortly after that the Cleveland Iron Mining Company took over the Marquette Company.

For half a decade the profitless struggle continued against the weather, reluctant workmen, cash shortage, harsh living, and very hard work building furnaces and plank roads and hauling ore from the mountain to the furnaces down winding Indian trails.

In 1853 J. J. St. Clair came on the scene as a mining agent. An energetic, analytical man, he was not on the iron range long before he realized that companies should not even consider making iron in the north. All food had to be imported expensively, including hay for the mules; weather and ice cut them off from the world six months each year; and the forest they were cutting down to charcoal the iron furnaces would soon be gone, and there was no coal nearby. Prepare to ship ore down to the lower Lakes for smelting, he

warned. Develop shipping. To test whether southern Ohio hard coal would make iron blooms as well as hardwood charcoal, St. Clair shipped south by laborious transport sample batches to meet lower Lakes' coal; four tons to Cincinnati via Cleveland and 152 tons to Pennsylvania furnaces.

The hard coal worked well with this ore from the northern mountain.

The *why* of bringing the ore down the Great Lakes for smelting was clear. But the *how* was not. The Upper Peninsula inland mines, Ishpeming and Negaunee, were an even harder downhill haul to the crude dock at Marquette. Even when a corduroy log road went in, it was hard to get a thousand tons a season down to the docks. One round trip from the mine to the smelter with 3,600 pounds of ore was a good day's work. The ore sleds often overran the mules on the slopes. The beleaguered Heman B. Ely's railroad replaced the mules, thus making it possible to bring down to the dock 1,200 tons a day.

However, the huge impasse was still the rapids at Sault Ste. Marie, or the Soo, in the St. Marys River, a white-water blockade to navigation. Portaging the vessels around the rapids was a Herculean feat. Sometimes vessels were hauled by columns of oxen out of Lake Superior and onto rollers. This huge parade then hauled the vessel right through the sometimes foot-deep mud of the main street and relaunched it below the falls.

At this pace, and with these costs, iron ore would come into the lower Lakes' ports as precious metal.

The Sleeping Plan

Long before the mineral wealth of the upper Lakes country was discovered, long-sighted trappers, commercial fishermen, and military men in the forest knew what huge commerce would be launched by a canal at the Soo to level the waters for ships.

As early as 1835, the pressure for a canal began. When U.S. troops stopped the state of Michigan from digging a canal in 1839, driving the workmen off, the pressure intensified against the federal government to authorize *and* fund a canal at Sault Ste. Marie. For ten years, waves of Western legislators, governors, and businessmen traveled to Washington to crash against an Eastern-dominated government, one hostile to Western improvements. Strangely enough, westerner Henry Clay led the opposition and tagged the canal proposal with his famous insult as "a work beyond the remotest settlement in the United States, if not [beyond] the moon."

The hammering finally broke through with canal legislation on August 21, 1852, enabling a canal "not less than 100 feet wide, 12 feet deep with two locks not less than 250 feet long." Work had to be started no later than 1855 and completed in ten years.

The construction of the Soo Canal was an American tour de force. The ant power of two thousand men and hundreds of oxen worked with crude tools sometimes in thirty-five-degrees-below-zero weather under the driving leadership of the indomitable Charles T. Harvey. Cholera struck down nearly two hundred men; work killed others.

But on April 19, 1855, Charles Harvey opened the sluice gate, and Lake Superior poured into the lock. Two ships locked through, the *Illinois* upbound and the *Baltimore* down. The canal had cost a million dollars; it would return billions. That June the two-masted brig *Columbia* locked down carrying on deck 120 tons of iron ore for the Cleveland Iron Mining Company. She tied up quietly at the Crawford & Price wharf in the Cuyahoga River. Only a handful suspected that they were watching the beginning of a continent's dominant waterborne commerce.

As with the Ohio Canal, the economic explosion following this canal was not evolutionary but immediate. Up to 1855 about 25,000 tons had been taken from all the Marquette

Range. In the second year after the canal's opening, 25,000 tons were shipped in a single season; in 1859, 68,832 tons; in 1860, 114,000 tons. In 1855, before the Soo Canal, the waterborne trip from Marquette to Cleveland was costing $3.00 per ton; in 1858 it cost $2.09 per ton. The toughest cost barrier had been broken.

The railroad-building era screamed for iron for rails. Sod-breaking homesteaders in the central plains needed the iron plow blades. Wagon builders were banding wheels with strap iron. A national population of 31 million needed iron.

Henry Chisholm came to Cleveland from Scotland nearly broke at age twenty, and eight years later he built the breakwater. Later he created Chisholm, Jones & Company to roll railroad iron. Iron was needed for steam engines, cooking ware, boiler plate, and a burgeoning era of machinery.

To meet this was a mountain of ore attracting lightning behind Marquette, Michigan, that could now be brought down the Lakes to smelters in Cleveland to meet coal coming north on the Ohio Canal.

And to convert the ore to iron blooms were a number of furnaces in Cleveland, Struthers, Youngstown, Niles, Akron, Elyria, Conneaut. Ashtabula, which found Michigan ore an excellent feed, already knew

that Mahoning County coal coked well.

Cleveland citizens appointed committees to study the city's economic future. In 1856, the committee reported that iron was the city's future. The public subscribed $60,000 for construction of a large blast furnace. Around the furnaces rose companies converting iron to product, for example, Otis and Ford (later Otis Iron and Steel) was making boiler plate and later cannons.

Other mining companies had made brave efforts on Michigan's harsh Upper Peninsula and had given up. What made the Cleveland Iron Mining Company endure was a remarkable group of Cleveland men who were not only business partners but personal friends.

Kindly, intellectual Dr. Morgan Hewitt, the company's first president, was interested in all sciences. That drew him and like-minded Cassels together. Hewitt was so dedicated to the operation that he moved his family from a luxury home in Cleveland to the rough lonesome mine area. Special friends of Hewitt were Samuel Mather and William J. Gordon. Gordon had come to Cleveland at age twenty-one to enter the grocery commission business on the Cuyahoga. By 1853 he had money to invest in iron mining. Selah Chamberlin came to Ohio in 1849 to build a railroad. He became a friend and next-door neighbor of Samuel Mather, who liked to assemble these men and others in his garden to talk science.

Among these vigorous entrepreneurs, the emerging central personality was Mather. Not an early president, he led from behind with a force of character that sustained operations during financial threats and calmed the organization during panics. He served as president from 1869 to 1890 and was succeeded by his son, William Gwinn Mather, who in 1950 was still coming to the office daily at age ninety-two.

Samuel L. Mather graduated with the first class of Connecticut Wesleyan University. He came to Cleveland in 1843 at age twenty-six to tend to his father's share of lands in the Connecticut Land Company. He found in the town an exciting group of doctors, lawyers, and commission merchants. When the rumors of minerals in Michigan's Upper Peninsula came downstream, Mather was one of a group of friends interested in investing in a speculation "beyond the moon."

And when the setbacks occurred, Mather was the one who calmly encouraged pouring more and more

dollars into what seemed a bottomless hole. When he could not get loans enough to cover surprise costs, he found other ways. For example, when the financial panic of 1857 drove iron furnaces and mines out of business, Mather and Gordon invented their own money for paying their miners. Nicely engraved certificates from $5.00 to $50.00 were redeemable against the company four months hence. Because of the reputation of Mather and the directors, these circulated at face value, just like real money. "Mr. Mather stands behind it." And over decades, what Mr. Mather stood behind would blossom. That would include several industries and scores of civic projects.

In 1861, the bombardment of Fort Sumter presaged feverish activity at the Cleveland port as the Cuyahoga Valley became Vulcan's workshop— filled with fire, furnace smoke, iron billets, and dangerous rolling mills. Cleveland, building railroads in all directions, needed iron. Wartime ordnance factories in Cleveland demanded iron.

That in turn required more and larger ships and more river and harbor facilities.

4

Cleveland Navy

On the water, the schooners were beautiful and fast; in port, clumsy and slow. The rigging snarled loading and unloading and stole cargo space. The largest schooner cargoes were generally under 400 tons.

In 1869, Eli Peck was making some sacrilegious drawings of a vessel designed specifically for the iron ore trade. To veteran marine people and to marine bankers, the design was ugly. The ship's pilot house sat way forward, practically on her bow so the captain could see the banks on narrow, curving channels. The engine and machinery were way aft, instead of amidships where it belonged. Between the pilot house and after housing was a long unobstructed deck, accessible for loading and unloading. Peck's vessel was a boxy, 211-foot trough.

While Peck had a very successful relationship with banks, this design was so unshiply that no bank would lend construction money. However, a practical Captain R. J. Hackett in Detroit saw the merits of this ugly duckling and became a financial partner, and his name went on the bow—the *R. J. Hackett*. The ship carried auxiliary sail *and* 1,200 tons of iron ore.

On the same design, Peck's yard next built another, the *Forest City*. There were no funds for an engine, so she operated as a towed consort to the *Hackett*. In one year the two vessels carried enough and profited enough to buy the *Forest City* an engine. These two vessels, the truest forerunners of the classic ore boat, later became beautiful in the eyes of beholders.

Steam had moved in, at first with auxiliary sail. But steam and sail worked side by side for many years, some schooners even working up to World War I and beyond. (The schooner *Our Son* operated until the 1930s.)

Ironsides

As far back as 1843 the navy sailed an ironclad on Lake Erie, the *Michigan*. Nineteen years later, the ironclad *Merchant* sailed out of Buffalo and worked successfully. In the winter of 1870–71 three famous 325-foot iron hulls were launched in Buffalo, dubbed "the big iron boats." They were the *China, India,* and *Japan,* the most popular passenger vessels on the Lakes for three decades.

The master of the *Japan* was twenty-six-year-old immigrant Alexander McDougall, who would later startle the marine community even more than Peck had by designing a radically shaped whaleback hull that would shed water and break ice and head waves. This design was so repugnant that, as with Peck's design, banks refused to fund it. Thus it was Rockefeller's man, Hoyt, who saw the merit and found the money. When McDougall's ugly "pig boat" took to the water, it performed so effectively

that it wiped out the laughter, and McDougall built forty-one whale-backs, many of which worked successfully well into the twentieth century. (One of them, the *Meteor,* worked into the 1950s as a tanker.)

Until 1882 the iron hulls were passenger ships. The first iron-hulled freighter was the 287-foot *Onoko,* launched in Cleveland. She was followed in 1884 by the steel-hulled *Spokane.* Steel then became the standard.

Steam and steel vessels grew in length and beam, each new vessel becoming "the largest on the Lakes." They were, of course, outgrowing the bottlenecks. The Soo Canal became too small, the St. Clair River too shallow, the docks too small, the unloaders too slow. And so a second round of canal and dock building and channel dredging began.

"I'll Talk to Ferris"

Flint-tough captains working under tonnage incentives bellowed for speed. It often required four or five days to unload a vessel.

Watching this pandemonium was J. D. Bothwell of Bothwell & Ferris. With forty horses for unloading schooners, he and his partner operated the old Hypano dock in Cleveland. Watching a gang of men driving piles to extend his dock, Bothwell noticed *how* they were doing it.

A small steam engine turned a

cable drum that lifted the piles into the air over the target and then dropped them.

He went to the shop of a couple of young engineers, Wallace, Parkhurst & Company, and asked Robert Wallace, "How much would you charge to build a small portable steam engine that I could move to any position on the dock to winch up a rope, lift a wash tub of iron ore out of a ship, then lower it onto the dock?"

"About $1,500."

"That's a lot of money. What if I supply the tub and cable?"

"Wouldn't change costs much."

"If I supply the frame, too?"

"The frame's not the . . ."

"If it works, there'll be a lot of engines needed."

"I'll talk to Parkhurst."

Wallace came back and said they would "attempt it for $1,200."

In 1867, $1,200 was still big money. Bothwell said, "I'll have to talk to Ferris."

When Bothwell and Ferris had their unloader in place, the first ship in was the 400-ton barque *Massillon* at 9:15 A.M., Captain Smith Moore commanding. He took a look at the little six-by-twelve engine and bellowed for horses.

Bothwell pleaded with the captain to give it a try. Moore reluctantly agreed to see how it went. A crowd of stevedores gathered along with crews of other vessels waiting to be unloaded. The engine sputtered alive.

The grins in the crowd disappeared when at ten o'clock that same night the *Massillon* was casting off, empty. All over the Cleveland docks men knew a new era had arrived.

Immediately Wallace and Parkhurst got orders for nine more engines. Bothwell and Ferris tried it next with three ore tubs attached. Stevedores were still needed, for all the engine did was repeatedly hoist three tubs into the hold. Shovelers filled the tubs. On the plank runway a wheeler and dumper kept the three ropes straight and signaled the engineer to hoist. The tubs were then dumped by the wheeler into the barrow that was pushed ashore on planks as before.

Bothwell and Ferris became wealthy. This system lasted until 1882.

While sail was still dominant, steam brought in important changes in everything from owner operation to fleet operation. Except for a few fleets like Bradley's, a schooner was often owned by its master and a few friends. But since steam required such a major investment for the engine, corporations entered boat ownership.

An Iron Ore Attitude

When the iron boom of the 1870s piled up ore on upper Great Lakes docks, captains would haul ore if they happened to be in the neighborhood and needed a cargo. Otherwise, captains said, no thanks to your piles of dirt that turned decks red and reddened sailors hands, which in turn reddened everything they touched, and then the crew spent hours washing down the vessels. Unloading the stuff required hours of hard labor. Crews often quit if they heard the next port was to load iron. Unloading tied up the vessel for days.

But Alva Bradley had a different attitude. He signed contracts to haul ore any time, any place. And he had the schooners to do it. In a single year (1875) he added six new ships for the iron ore trade and was able to make long-term transportation contracts. His vessel masters regarded him with profound respect.

By the time other captains discovered that hauling iron ore was a giant market, Bradley owned it and set the rates. Very early he had recognized that wooden schooners were too small and too slow and had moved to steam and steel.

Bradley died in 1885, but his descendants continued to expand the Bradley shipping and business empire that grew out of a cook's assistant's berth on a small vessel out of Vermilion.

Formation of a Giant

In 1865 John Parkhurst and Robert Wallace had a small machine shop on the east bank of the Cuyahoga. Three years later they bought Globe Iron Works, which had been making ship machinery for a dozen years. The purchasing company assumed the good Globe name and in a series of further acquisitions became such a successful shipbuilder, their vessels in such demand, that they had to move their yard to the head of the Old River Bed. There they could build four steel freighters simultaneously.

In 1888 the Ship Owners Dry Dock Company organized on Waddell Street in the Old River Bed. Veteran shipbuilder W. H. Radcliffe was the prime mover. The company officers were well-known Cleveland names: Captain Thomas Wilson; M. A. Bradley, Alva's son; H. D. Goveder; Gustave Cold; George L. Quayle. Further consolidation saw Globe Iron Works purchase the Cleveland Dry Dock Company in 1899.

In 1886, Robert Wallace and Henry D. Coffinberry created the Cleveland Shipbuilding Company and bought the old Cuyahoga Steam Furnace site. They built yards facing the river as well as a plant in Lorain that had the largest dry docks on the Lakes.

In March 1899, the whole "thing" came together under the umbrella of the American Ship Building Company, which purchased facilities of Cleveland Shipbuilding, the Globe Works, the Ship Owners Dry Dock, and yards in Buffalo, Detroit, Milwaukee, West Superior, West Bay

City, and Chicago. The company's headquarters was on West 59th Street in Cleveland.

The Alexander Brown

On the Great Lakes you will see the name Brown on vessels and machinery. Fayette Brown and his son, Harvey, were in mining and ships. Brown's other son, Alexander, built bridges. Watching the laborious process of discharging an ore ship, Alexander saw that what they needed was a bridge. He invented a series of movable towers with arms bridging out from the dock over the open hatches of ships. Cables conveyed a bucket from the hold across an ore bridge to railroad cars or stockpiles ashore. Each such Brown Hoist had three movable towers.

The system worked fast, and suddenly the thinning forest of vessel masts in the ports was thick again, this time with unloader towers. These Brown unloaders were installed side by side, as close as they could pack the ships, at every dock. Brown improved upon this with his steam operated Brown Bridge Tramway.

Men still had to load the tub by hand until Mason, of Mason and Hoover, soon thereafter invented the clamshell-type Mason Bucket, which, when pulled, closed its grab on the ore. When the tub disappeared from the docks in favor of the clamshell, larger ships could unload at the docks. This in turn made the Soo Canal too small.

The Bucket That Changed the Ports

In 1898 a phenomenal 13.6 million tons of iron ore—the largest vessels carrying 7,500 tons—came down the Great Lakes, thus overwhelming the unloading systems in Cleveland. At that time, longshoremen in the hold at unloading time were paid a dime per ton of ore shoveled into buckets. A man could shovel ten tons a day.

Mild-mannered materials handling engineer George H. Hulett had an idea for a machine that would revolutionize unloading. It would be very expensive to build. Hulett's friends went to Andrew Carnegie to ask him to buy it for unloading his ore at Conneaut. The shrewd Scot listened to the advantages and made his counterproposal: they could build it on their own, and if it worked he would buy it.

Work proceeded throughout 1898 on the homeliest monster dock workers had ever seen. A huge elbow stuck up in the sky; on the end of the arm was a huge hand that was guided by a man seated in the wrist. The operator could revolve the hand 360 degrees to scrape the vessel hold clean. The upper arm was attached to a traveling base on rails, which enabled the whole rig to back up and dump the load into a railroad car or a stockpile. The whole cycle required only two minutes.

While the monster was ready for the 1899 iron ore season, there were problems to be expected with such a complex innovation, the first being that no one wanted to ride on the wrist of the machine to operate it.

The measure of the machine's success was determined when Andrew Carnegie and Charles Schwab visited the dock to inspect the Hulett unloader in action. Carnegie paid his bill and ordered four more Huletts.

The importance of this unloader cannot be overstated. William Livingston, president of Lake Carriers' Association said, "The thing that most influenced the change in type and size of bulk freighters . . . [was] the invention of the Hulett unloader." Indeed, the Hulett started another revolution in port and harbor operations.

5

The Long Ships

Approaching 1890, the bulk carriers widened and deepened and, especially, lengthened. Landsmen were surprised to find they could walk alongside a ship at the pier for the length of four hundred-foot house lots. For the close-up viewer the vast sides shut out all reference points, so it seemed that the ship stood still and the dock moved. Viewed when approaching dead-on, it appeared that these giants did not move; rather, they loomed toward the dock.

Captains competed for cargoes, raced each other to get first in line at fuel docks, loading docks, the Soo locks, and unloading docks. Few had time or incentive for concern about the collective welfare of the industry beyond the next channel marker.

However, a cluster of Cleveland vessel owners, builders, and users rendezvoused on September 1, 1880, as the Cleveland Vessel Owners Association. It remained little more than a conversation club until 1887, when M. A. Bradley became president, H. M. Hanna vice president, and B. L. Pennington secretary.

Meanwhile, over in Philadelphia a heavily mustached Franklin J. Firth had a large view of Great Lakes commerce. Buffalo transportation men were accustomed to listening to Firth's suggestions, and he was accustomed to having them listen. "One day en route to a Chicago conference, I thought it advisable to unite the Buffalo, Erie and other rail and lake lines in an association to take in all competing lake lines. I drafted a constitution and by-laws on the train and secured their adoption at Chicago."

S. D. Caldwell was the first president of this resulting Lake Carriers' Association, and Firth became its president in 1899.

Competitors Cooperate?

Members of Lake Carriers' focused objectives in a general meeting in Chicago on February 16, 1881: "The object . . . [is] devising and discussing plans for the protection of the interests of lake tonnage, steam or sail." The organization further stated the purpose of the Buffalo organization: "To consider and take action upon all general questions relating to the navigation and carrying business of the Great Lakes and the waters tributary thereto, with the intent to improve . . . service . . . to protect the common interests of the Lake carriers and to promote their general welfare." Of prime importance to both the Cleveland and Buffalo organizations was the character of service rendered.

The groups worked separately on matters such as reciprocity in wrecking privileges, establishing aids to navigation, and improving channels; but they joined forces when strength was needed, for example, to successfully oppose the bridging of the Detroit River and the Load Line Bill in Congress.

Their opposition to this legislation was not intended to ignore safety. But the organizations knew that this particular bill would disastrously affect many classes of lake vessels. Later, the association voluntarily established load lines without legislation.

These joint ventures made obvious the desirability for a closer working relationship between the two organizations. Finally, on April 28, 1892, representatives of shipping interests from all parts of the Great Lakes gathered in Detroit and merged the Buffalo and Cleveland groups into one Lake Carriers' Association, with M. A. Bradley president. Invitations to join went out to all Great Lakes vessel owners. The association's headquarters was in Cleveland.

To help assure unity and prevent splintering into local groups, the Association limited the president's term to one year and required representation from many different ports on the board. Despite the one-year presidency rule, the men who followed M. A. Bradley in that office between 1895 and 1902 managed to keep the Association on a straight course: Thomas Wilson, Cleveland; William Livingstone, Detroit; Captain J. J. H. Brown, Buffalo; James W. Millen, Detroit; Captain James S. Dunham, Chicago; Franklin J. Firth, Philadelphia; William C. Farrington, Buffalo; Captain A. B. Wolvin, Duluth.

Down to Business

Initially, the officers sought out agricultural interests and worked to pass the Rivers and Harbors Bill, which provided for dredging twenty-foot channels west of Buffalo. They successfully pushed the Brickner Lighthouse Bill responsible for building many new lighthouses. And by drafting and enforcing new passing rules in narrow channels, they reduced the number of collisions. As early as 1891, the Association actively opposed tolling domestic waterways. And in 1895 it studied the effect of the Chicago drainage canal on Lakes levels.

The Lake Carriers' Association established strategic lake port shipping offices, successfully maintained fair fuel rates, and effected economies in grain handling. They obtained government compliance in rules for navigating the St. Marys River and encouraged the War Department to create safeguards for passage through the more difficult sections of the West Neebish Channel approach to the Soo, better known as "the Rock Cut," a devil of a trip.

Reorganization

In 1903, the Association reorganized and expanded objectives to include establishing shipping offices for the securing of seamen; establishing and maintaining aids to navigation; improving channels, docks, wharves, and loading and unloading facilities; maintaining amicable relations between employers and employees and thus avoiding lockouts or strikes.

Milestones

Following that 1903 reorganization, William Livingstone, newly elected Association president, provided inspired leadership and tireless energy through his twenty-three-year term. So much for term limits.

In 1904, another Detroit man, George A. Marr, joined as secretary. He became secretary-treasurer in 1919 and vice president in 1929 and continued to guide the Association for more than forty years with such contributions as the Association's winter school program and the seamen's savings plan.

In 1909, the Association established its Welfare Plan, one of the earliest industry-wide projects to promote employer-employee amity.

Despite its casual beginning, the Lake Carriers' Association became the most powerful association of vessel owners in the United States.

The Fleet

Crossing the century marker into the 1900s, the Great Lakes vessels grew to 500 feet with the construction of the *Isaac L. Ellwood*, and bulk commerce was booming.

Rockefeller's Bessemer fleet numbered sixty vessels. The fleets of Cleveland-Cliffs, Federal Steel, and Lake Superior Iron numbered sixty more. Beyond those were a dozen smaller fleets crowding the channels.

Loading docks grew so that whole trains of hopper-bottom railcars could now run onto them to dump into the loading bins above the chutes on twenty-four-foot centers.

Iron ore mining pushed westward from the Marquette Range to the Gogebic, the Cuyuna, and up beyond the head of the Lakes, where the wild and famous Merritt Brothers owned kingdoms of Minnesota pine forests growing over 65 percent ore lying ready to take for scuffing aside a few centuries of pine needles on the vast Mesabi Range. (Later, the former Cleveland oil man would show the iron men the value of this range. While they haggled, he bought it. With his ships and his iron range, Rockefeller could set the prices.) And north of the Mesabi was the Vermilion Range and the Steep Rock District.

Costs rocketed. Consider only the minor item—horses. It cost $650 to work one horse for one year; and there were 350 horses working the mines. Power shovels were just coming into use, but their breakdown rate kept horses in the mines.

Ships grew . . . again. The large vessels of the late nineteenth century were obsolete by 1904, when a new generation of ships, like the first *William G. Mather,* began carrying 10,700 tons.

When World War I required all the steel we could make, a still larger class arrived in 1917 with the *Pontiac,* which carried 13,500 tons.

The Great Lakes needed more bulk carriers, but the ore people had to compete with the U.S. government and foreign nations, both of which overloaded Great Lakes yards with orders for warships, with the U.S. alone ordering 445 vessels built. Consequently, new shipyards opened on the Lakes.

1100 Terminal Tower

Pandemonium developed at all ports. Downbound vessels stood in line at lower Lakes ports waiting to be unloaded. Railroads bringing coal north to meet certain ships were in a traffic jam waiting for vessels to unload. Sometimes the vessel they were to load with coal went to a different port to get out of traffic. Railroads not only had to divert trains to other ports, causing great waste and confusion, but they also needed to see that the right type of hopper cars were at the right ports. Often one company's upbound boat sailed empty when another company's urgent upbound cargo sat waiting at a dock for an available boat.

This enormous confusion and waste screamed for a central coordinating dispatch system. And so the Ore and Coal Exchange was born to match up vessels with cargoes and unloaders and ports and railroads. Since vessel and railroad companies were based in Cleveland, the headquarters was established at 1100 Terminal Tower. The results were dramatic.

Daily at noon, dispatchers from the coal and ore and vessel and railroad companies all met to coordinate shipments. As they left the dining room, they stopped by the central dispatcher's office and filed the arrangements they had made with other companies for movement of cargoes.

The Ore and Coal Exchange continued after the war, and even today dispatchers receive regular position radio reports from all carriers in motion on the water and rail to keep order at the ports. The dispatcher can make destination shifts and cargo changes swiftly for efficient use of ports, rails, and boats.

Working the Docks in the 1930s

The vessels developed in the 1920s were more than adequate to handle the low-volume depression decade of the 1930s. Trees grew up in the dry docks. Docks in Cleveland were hungry for work.

What was it like to be a longshoreman on the docks of the Cuyahoga River in the middle of the Great Depression? Twenty percent of the population was out of work. The fortunate ones had either full- or part-time work.

Wages were on the floor: 20 cents an hour was common; if you had a skilled job, you might make 90 cents an hour. The highest salaried people in the country, presidents of steel or automobile companies, drew $50,000 per year. Baseball players made $11,000 (except for superstars like Babe Ruth); professional football players made up to $10,000. During this period, longshoremen were fairly high up the scale, earning between 60 and 75 cents per hour. Elite crane operators made 90 cents. These were good jobs when work was available. But, because of the ice, shipping in Cleveland usually started in April and ended by December 1—a short year.

The main cargoes were, of course, iron ore and stone, but there were also cargoes from overseas—sulfur, phosphate rock, potash, copper ingots, scotch whiskey, cement, asphalt, and other raw materials.

As a dock worker in Cleveland at that time, I can attest to what life was like. First we would hear about a ship coming in, usually from our union or by word of mouth from other longshoremen. Most likely we would then take a streetcar or bus to Public Square and then walk down to the flats to the dock where the ship was expected. We would wait there until the dock superintendent started hiring, knowing that we would be considered only for this one ship. Most of the time there were a couple hundred men waiting; only about forty-five would be selected.

If one of the men was lucky, he would be told what shift he would work (they unloaded the ship twenty-four hours a day). He would then either start to work immediately or come back at the designated time.

If the ship was loaded with sulfur or potash or phosphate rock, he would probably be sent into the hold to shovel the clean (material the crane could not reach) up into the crane bucket.

Other potential jobs would be fireman on one of the cranes (run by hand-fired steam boilers) or signalman, directing the crane operator where to put his bucket, how far down in the hold to go, and when to reposition the ship to reach remaining cargo.

When the crane loaded the material into a gondola or hopper freight car, a man was needed to position the car, help move the loaded car to the switching track, and bring back an empty car for loading. The cranes were locomotive types that rode rails.

Sulfur and the potash especially were hard to work; the men work with covered noses and mouths with kerchiefs leaving the eyes to take the dust. Masks were unavailable; safety goggles were uncommon. Men wore heavy clothes to keep the chemicals away from their bodies. If it rained or blew, the work went on, and the day was long.

These three materials—sulfur, potash, and phosphate—came to Cleveland in large ships from Mexico, Germany, and Spain and off-loaded on the East Coast into self-propelled barges that came up the Hudson River to the Erie Canal and then west to Lake Erie. There was no seaway. Some came straight here in small tramp steamers without having to be reloaded. Barnes Barge Lines was one of the biggest carriers. The material went to make fertilizer for the American Agricultural Chemical Company and Grasselli Chemical Company, later DuPont.

Other materials—copper ingots, scotch, cement, asphalt—came in the same type of ships, but the unloading was different. The cement came in ninety-four-pound bags and had to be manually handled onto a pallet, picked up by a crane, and moved by hand to conveyer into a warehouse where it again was stacked up for loading onto trucks at a later time. And of course, it could not be unloaded in rain because it would harden.

The copper had to be moved from the hold ingot by ingot; each weighed between 1,500 and 2,000 pounds. The men in the hold put steel cables at each end; then the crane hoisted them onto railroad flat cars. If ingots were small enough to be handled by men and hand dollies, they usually went into boxcars.

The asphalt came from Trinidad and was loaded by crane and bucket, usually onto a pile at the dock where it could be reloaded onto trucks. The whiskey came in cases that were hand loaded onto pallets and then onto conveyers and into a warehouse. (This was very carefully watched by U.S. Customs for thievery. Even so, when an occasional case dropped, the contents quickly disappeared.)

All loading had to be done very carefully in order to protect the workers from serious accidents.

Most ships were small and able to unload in two or three days. The longshoreman earned $25 to $35 per ship, with some overtime, and were paid in cash from a Brinks armored truck. Later they were paid by check, though they much preferred the cash. The men were generally thirty to forty years of age and experienced. Later on, some were asked to take regular steady jobs but refused; they liked the independence of spot work. There were many Irish, Polish, and Pennsylvania Dutch. Very often whole families of sons came to Cleveland for this work. Dock workers were all hard workers and temperamental. They almost always had nicknames, their real names seldom known except on the pay sheets.

One day a man came running into the office of the stevedoring company very upset. The plug of tobacco he had started to chew contained a human thumb. He wasn't particularly worried about whose thumb it was; he wanted to know how he could get his money back from the store that sold it!

The Cuyahoga River at that time was a disgrace. Usually covered with oil, logs, and floating debris of all kinds, the river's temperature was over 110 degrees. Methane bubbles from the bottom broke the surface and could be ignited. There wasn't much of a fuss about it; most people just accepted it. Every year a contract was let to dredge it; this took all summer and fall. The dredgings were dumped into the lake about three and a half miles out at a designated spot. This obviously just moved the oil and chemical scum and debris into the lake. Moving the pollution was the solution.

All along the river, the docks were in various degrees of repair—some good but many in very poor shape with good-sized holes back under the piling. Some of these holes were homes to the indigent who carried crates and set them up under the pilings so that they could live and sleep near a warm river and near the factories where they could salvage junk metal and cans to sell for food money.

Of course, they shared their caves with rats and all kinds of debris. They never bathed and were terrible looking. One man's cave caught fire one night and he had to be taken to the hospital for burns. While there, they bathed him. After his release several days later, he complained that he had skin problems because of the bath. These hermits never caused a problem. They had no names, no relations, no worldly possessions.

The flats along the river were thought to be very dangerous. Only those who worked a night shift went that way at night on foot. You avoided anyone when walking the streets. If you heard someone coming toward you, you crossed to the other side of the street. If you didn't, he usually did. If he did not, you assumed you were in for a fight. This did not happen too often, but it was still a dangerous place.

There were three famous bars in the flats. The Flat Iron Cafe on Center Street, Jim's at Scranton Road, and the Hole on Jefferson. They all served fair food and policed their patrons, which included every walk of life from suburban people slumming to the dock and factory workers.

The flats in 1935 was a fascinating and very different place than it is now. The big mills, chemical plants, refineries, grain mills, machine shops, foundries, and lumber mills were there. In a way, it was the real working heart of the city. Today, most big industry has been displaced.

The lakefront in the 1930s had several docks beside the main ore docks. These handled construction aggregates, newsprint, and a lot of passenger traffic that came in at East 9th Street.

Passenger ships from Detroit and Buffalo ran regularly and the cruise ships like the *North America* and *South America* called weekly with tours up to Georgian Bay and occasionally a trip to Mackinac Island. The largest passenger ship was the *Seeandbee,* which could sleep 1,500 and carry 6,000 passengers. With six decks, 510 staterooms, and twenty-four parlors, and its engines delivering 12,000 horsepower, the *Seeandbee* came regularly to Cleveland. (She later became the navy training carrier USS *Wolverine.*)

The Nicholson Terminal at East 55th Street and Cleveland Builders at East 40th Street were the main docks on the lakefront, except for the Pennsylvania Ore Dock. Some of the passenger vessels were luxury liners with deluxe staterooms and ornate salons and superb white-tablecloth dining.

As World War II loomed, the depression on the docks waned. Traffic into the Cleveland Harbor and up the river became heavy in the late 1930s. The largest lake freighters were in the

600-foot class. They could go up the Cuyahoga with two tugs and a lot of care. If they were going to the Pennsylvania Ore Dock or Cleveland Builders with stone, the boats had no problems and needed no tug unless the wind was up, especially from the northeast or west.

On some days eight or ten ships came in, plus two or three passenger boats and a couple of foreign ships or barges. The harbor master usually let one freighter come up the river at the same time that another one was coming down and several were being loaded or unloaded. This meant from April to December there was a constant use of the harbor and the river. During World War II, the traffic was critical for national defense, and any interruption of it would have been disastrous. The construction boom following the war was also dependent on these cargoes of stone, sand, and ore.

World War II on the Docks

Leading into World War II, the Great Lakes bulk fleet was inadequate. Pittsburgh Steamship commissioned five new ships, each with capacities ranging from 15,000 to 17,500 tons. The Maritime Commission ordered sixteen more, each able to carry 260 railroad carloads, and these vessels were sold to the iron ore and shipping companies. The ships carried traveling cranes that could uncover

eighteen hatches in thirteen minutes. The engine rooms had automatic stokers, since the shovel-handling fireman was on the way out. To furnish the war with steel, Cleveland shipping offices directed by radio phone an upbound and downbound parade of vessels—up with coal and down with iron ore.

The war screamed for ships, and shipbuilders screamed for the steel to build them. Competing for steel to build the Lake fleet were orders for 200 oceangoing cargo ships, the all-welded Liberty ships, mine sweepers, and destroyers. The Great Lakes ore companies took to converting automobile carriers to bulk vessels. And in order to fill demand, the ore fleet sailed earlier than usual and ran later into winter, raising the risk and further burdening all support installations.

The Peace Threat

The war ended in August 1945 with the U.S. and Canadian fleets panting for repairs. Having brought down nearly a half billion tons of ore and having moved unprecedented masses of coal, stone, and grain, vessels were running on cobbled-up machinery and standby gear. There were then 335 U.S. flag vessels, not counting Canadians. Many of these had been converted from other uses and were converted back to original use, leaving 261 U.S. bulk vessels, with an average age of thirty-two years. Seventy-three of these were old timers carrying less than 9,000 tons that were actually obsolete; another forty carried under 10,000 tons.

Vessel owners, however, reasonably felt that the economy could revert to the depression of the 1930s; hence, they did not rush into new construction. However, nearly everyone underestimated the impact of a breakout of peace. With no more rationing, John Q. Public could take the eight-year-old Studebaker out onto the turnpike and really open her up. When the public did this en masse, tires blew, fan belts broke, radiators sprayed the engines, and brakes faded. And in the houses, refrigerators and ranges broke down. War brides wanted to move out of the in-laws' houses, so huge residential developments sprung up. These developments were like new towns, and each required its own shopping center and utilities. Added to this was

Truman and Marshall's decision to feed and rebuild Europe before Stalin had a chance to starve them into the Soviet Union.

As vessel owners placed orders for ships, *demand for steel exploded.*

Ships aren't built in a day. On September 15, 1950, before shipbuilders could much alleviate the demand for ore, U.S. troops swarmed ashore at Inchon, Korea. The new war was on. And more steel was needed. The new generation of bulk carriers was 647-footers with 70-foot beams and 36-feet molded depth and carrying nearly 20,000 tons, as typified by the *Philip R. Clarke, Arthur M. Anderson,* and the *Carson J. Callaway.*

In the mid-1950s a new generation of still-larger vessels was being planned to meet the maximum length and beam that could navigate the highly anticipated St. Lawrence Seaway. These included vessels like the 728-foot *Fitzgerald.*

6

Prelude to the Port Authority

The St. Lawrence Seaway

"The final all-clear signal goes from me to Dr. Holden at 0800. He'll push the button. I want an all-clear call from each of your sections by 0730 telling me there's nobody within a quarter mile of the stakes."

"That's more than the project code reads."

"This river can't read."

On June 30, 1958, sun-leathered field engineer Del E. W. Smythe had no fear of explosives, high-iron construction, or top brass. But water was something else. And this would be more water than most engineers ever tried to control. He was ten hours away from the instant when Dr. Otto Holden would fire thirty tons of explosives, blowing the cofferdam up-stream and releasing a twenty-foot tidal wave through the dry lake bed to slam up against the new power dam twenty-five miles downstream at Cornwall-Massena. It would create the new Lake St. Lawrence, completing what was then man's most audacious hydraulic project: deep-keel navigation to the sea—the St. Lawrence Seaway.

Smythe went through the entire list of contractors, subcontractors, consultants, architects, and utilities involved. Were these people all out from in front of the 310,000 cubic feet per second of water that would be unleashed?

"Sir, Dr. Emerson's archaeologists ask for just five more hours."

"No. Out!"

"They found another layer, sir.

Indian pottery. Said it would be lost forever under the water."

"*Pot*-tery?"

"Yes, sir. With designs like some found in Siberia. Said it would help prove the link between Asia and . . ."

Smythe put up the flat of his hand. "Three hours—period! Pottery or not!"

Thousands of people were arriving to watch the great wave break loose. Smythe asked for more police. Crossing his mind occasionally was the thought that some children might make a pilgrimage back into the cut for a last look at the site of their previous homes and towns. Many children had difficulty understanding.

But there was worse on Smythe's mind. All calculations had been tested on the model. When the dam was blown, the waters of the Great Lakes should fill the new Lake St. Lawrence—only—and then stop. But veteran engineers had come to a mystical respect for the rampaging St. Lawrence, which had defeated man's best efforts at control and deep-water navigation. The river had startled them frequently during construction, spinning their cofferdams like revolving doors, rolling twenty-ton boulders out of dikes, melting mountains of sand.

They calculated that the blowout would only gently lower Lake Ontario an inch and raise Montreal harbor two and one-half inches, but they wondered some nights whether it would wash out the planned shore-line, find soft spots to make channels of its own, skirt the dam, overflow it, drain Ontario too fast and ground vessels upstream (or downstream), blast vessels loose from moorings at Montreal, and deluge shore villages.

Tomorrow they would know.

Four years earlier, the world really had not known what the St. Lawrence Seaway was. The citizens of Iroquois, Canada, and several other towns learned about the seaway when they heard repeatedly that their towns would have to be moved; then plans were canceled. They had shrugged it off. This one would also fail, "*C'est ca.*"

Navigationally ice-locked during the white months and rapids-blocked during the green, the potentially greatest inland waterway in the world frustrated commerce for four hundred years. Boulder-churning rapids denied deep-keel traffic to the sea.

The proposed twenty-seven-foot-deep seaway would cut shipping costs $22.50 per ton from midcontinent to Europe by reducing the number of tolls. Far beyond that, the big savings would be the nonstop trip to the sea, cutting out the unloading and re-loading into smaller vessels to bypass rapids and then the reloading into ocean vessels.

Making this St. Lawrence outlet to the sea navigable would require deep slack-water canals around the rapids, with stair-step locks from Thousand Islands down to Montreal. Add to that a few more locks and canals and deepened ports on the upper Lakes, and one could float thirty thousand tons from Duluth to the ocean.

While the Americans working on the project generally felt that they were pioneering, all Canadians have always been historians; therefore, Del Smythe knew that he was actually working on an old, old dream.

Captain Jacques Cartier, steering for China in the spring of 1534, was blocked by the Lachine Rapids. In 1689 a great engineering-minded cleric, Dollier de Casson, began digging a foot-and-a-half-deep canal around the Lachine Rapids. But the Iroquois's mystic reverence for the mighty St. Lawrence tolerated no man-made interference with it. Casson's men had two thousand yards hacked out of stone when one August night a war party fell on the workers and butchered them.

Canal work stopped until 1700, when the Sulpician priests hired contractor Gideon de Cathlogne to complete the project. But money ran out, and the rapids remained boss for seventy-five more years.

The American Revolution spurred the first sustained drive to make the St. Lawrence into a seaway. Canadian colonists had made the pivotal decision to reject the American colonies' invitations to send delegates to Phila-delphia, so the rebelling American colonies, fearing an ally of the king next door, attacked across the St. Lawrence and seized Montreal, the capital of the North American fur trade.

The following spring the English successfully counterattacked, but the event convinced Quebec's governor in chief, Frederick Haldimand, that in the event of war with the colonies, Canada would not be able to move her troops or supply them unless she could navigate around the St. Lawrence rapids on her own side. Haldimand's first move detailed the Royal Engineers to build a linkage of small canals to bypass the most hazardous Lachine Rapids in the twelve miles joining Lake St. Francis to Lake St. Louis (wide places in the St. Lawrence). He began with the Coteau Rapids, which bar the upstream progress from Montreal into Lake St. Francis and where he had seen eighty-four men killed. This Coteau Canal was nine hundred feet long, seven feet wide, and two and a half feet deep and had three locks, each under forty feet long, built of stone masonry by Cornish miners. While dangerous, the Coteau Rapids were nevertheless navigable by flat-bottomed boats.

The third white-water stairway was the Split Rock Rapids. Here a series of three small canals was built, the Faucile, the Trou du Moulin, and the Split Rock. Completed in 1783, these were almost immediately inadequate. A revolution in trade goods was floating into Montreal. Fur from the north and upper Lakes was augmented by wheat, flour, and timber. The canoe was waning on the upper St. Lawrence in favor of bateaux, scows, and Durham boats. The Durham was a shallow-draft scow, but it had a keel and centerboard that needed water underneath.

The War of 1812 sparked the real action against the rapids. Long convoys of barges heading west with military goods for British forts on the upper St. Lawrence and Great Lakes clogged the meager canal system and were delayed by the rapids. The British naval shipbuilding base at Kingston suffered serious supply delay, threatening British-Canadian defense.

An absence of deep canals carried still another threat—an economic one. United States leaders were already considering an incredible canal that would reach from Lake Erie at Buffalo east to Albany and the Hudson River, a canal on which cargoes could float south to the port of New York and then to Europe at the same time that Canadian cargoes were blocked by rapids, thus cutting Montreal and Quebec out of the trade.

Lower Canada built a new Lachine Canal, completed in 1825. For the first time some of the river's worst rapids could be bypassed by vessels big enough to carry a good payload. In that same year, however, New York completed its spectacular Erie Canal from Lake Erie to the Hudson and New York City.

In 1833, when the Erie Canal was floating many times the St. Lawrence tonnage in wheat and flour, the competitive Upper Canada legislature voted $280,000 to improve four distinct series of rapids between Montreal and Prescott and for vessels not of three-foot draft but of nine. This was the first really coordinated master plan hinting at an eventual St. Lawrence Seaway.

But always there was the formidable Niagara. As early as 1824, a daring promoter, William Hamilton Merritt, began a fantastic project upstream at the unconquerable navigation barrier. He was a good engineer, a fair businessman, and a superb salesman. Merritt formed the Welland Canal Company based on an audacious plan: a nine-mile canal of forty locks, each 100 feet long and 8 feet deep, to skirt Niagara and drop vessels 326 feet from Lake Erie to the Welland River below the falls.

On November 30, 1829, two brigantines of seven-and-a-half-foot draft walked up the forty locks. St. Lawrence navigation had reached from the Atlantic to Lake Erie.

By 1850 the tiny Canadian population had completed the unbelievable—a full set of canals and locks enabling at least nine-foot navigation all the way from Montreal up the St. Lawrence, around Niagara, across Lake Erie, up the Detroit River, across Lake St. Clair, and on into Lake Huron.

The last remaining obstacle was the rapids at Sault Ste. Marie. As with the Welland, this also required a salesman, American William Fairbanks, who built the Soo Canal (St. Mary's Falls Canal) at Sault Ste. Marie. In 1856 nine-foot navigation was open from the Atlantic to Duluth.

All hands had barely finished congratulating themselves when new vessels required fourteen feet. When Canada's provinces confederated in 1867, the new federal government deepened the St. Lawrence canals to fourteen feet. This program required a quarter century, and the canals were used for sixty years.

When the ice thawed in 1901, men talked vehemently of bringing deep-draft ocean ships into mid-America. The big iron-ore, coal, and limestone shippers were not interested in seeing foreign-flag vessels bring in Europe's competing steel products. But others wanted outbound wheat to reach the ocean without reloading twice. A cry rose for twenty-feet of water on the St. Lawrence route.

The governments of Canada and the United States appointed an International Waterway Commission to study the feasibility of this project. A favorable report was made quickly but came up hard against a formidable coalition. Coal and oil companies feared competition from the hydroelectric potential of the St. Lawrence. East Coast and Gulf Coast ports wailed that a deep-water channel to the heart of the continent would leave them ghost ports. Eastern business feared that the seaway would shift the financial-industrial center of gravity westward. Railroaders felt that seaway competition would bankrupt them. Together these forces defeated the joint U.S.-Canadian seaway proposals under Coolidge and again under Hoover and Roosevelt.

In the 1950s, the U.S. anti-seaway lobby was as virulent as ever, but it was suddenly outflanked by Canada. The House of Commons decided to go it alone. The result was immediate. Suddenly there was concern that Canada would have all the electric power to itself. Also, there was a postwar shortage of direct shipping ore from the upper Lakes and new interest in Labrador ore. Faced with a possible all-Canadian seaway, Americans decided to favor U.S.-Canada seaway plans.

A political war broke out on the U.S. side over size of the locks. Cleveland's George Humphrey of M. A. Hanna Company was a long-sighted man who even then predicted 1,000-foot-long, 75-feet-wide ore carriers. Having helped Truman push through the Marshall Plan, he was secretary of treasury and an influence in the Seaway negotiations. He pushed for lock capacity for thousand-foot boats. However, Eastern seaboard ports did not want ocean cargoes diverted to Great Lakes ports. Congress held the lock size down to accommodate 730 foot ships. That excluded all but five hundred ships in the world from entering the Seaway. To accommodate the majority of ships, locks should have been 1,000 feet long and 150 feet wide.

For the hydroelectric project, 18,000 U.S. acres between Waddington and Massena and 20,000 Canadian acres between Iroquois and Cornwall had to be flooded. These included eighteen cemeteries, ten villages, and the homes of eight thousand people.

Giant house-moving machines transported each house so gently that china was left in cupboards. A glass of water was placed on the kitchen table so that the owner could judge whether the house had had a smooth move. As the house moved inland, its favorite shrubs followed in the next transport. Moreover, if its owners wanted it to stand next door to its century-old neighbor, that too was arranged.

As bulldozers moved onto the largest North American engineering project ever undertaken by men, a feat of precision scheduling challenged the presumptuous engineers.

On the International Rapids section alone, for example, the new hydroelectric dams would inundate Canada's existing fourteen-foot canal system. The engineers must time operations so that the old fourteen-foot traffic could continue during the construction years. When the new locks were ready, traffic must be able to switch over immediately upon inundation of the old canals.

Tampering successfully with a powerful river lined with millions of homes and scores of cities requires precision. A three-inch error in the water level could turn a town into an island or, conversely, ground a hundred ships. Twelve enormous scale models were made to predict downstream effects.

Fleets of graders, scrapers, bulldozers, earthmovers, and draglines clanked in.

Hydroelectrically, the mission on the stretch called the International Rapids section was to change the gradual eighty-five-foot drop of the rapids into a steep drop at a single point. The St. Lawrence River would be dammed to turn the rapids into a twenty-five-mile lake; then it would be plunged eighty-five feet over turbine blades at Cornwall at a rate of 110 million gallons per minute.

To build this seaway section with its canals, locks, dams, two electric generating stations, dikes, and embankments, 100 million cubic yards of dirt would have to be moved, a third of it from underwater. Four million yards of concrete would be poured; 20,000 tons of structural iron would be raised; and 20,000 tons of gates and hoists would be built. Long Sault Dam alone called for thirty vertical-lift sluice gates, as wide and high as houses, to be raised and lowered by traveling crane hoists of 275-ton capacity. Twenty miles of dikes would be built.

Cofferdams were built at both ends of the twenty-five-mile valley to hold the river out so that contractors could work mostly in the dry. Tunnels were driven under the old fourteen-foot canal so that earthmovers could get to the new work site without interrupting vessel traffic.

Regulating the outflow from Lake Ontario would be the new Iroquois Dam, which had two 350-ton traveling cranes to open and close its thirty-two gates. For ships to bypass these two dams, two new locks were required, the Eisenhower and the Snell.

Looking at the feverish activity in the great cut, the curious public could see no outline of what was being built. It looked instead like a confused battleground as different contractors and subcontractors simultaneously built the power dams, powerhouses, control dams, levees, canals, locks, and dikes. But men like Del Smythe in the engineering building saw the blueprint behind the confusion.

In the middle of operations, in 1957, on the American side of the cut alone, the working fleet was composed of 135 shovels and draglines, 400 crawler tractors, 730 trucks, eight dredges, and 14,000 men—all watched by a half million fascinated visitors.

One day in July, Dr. Norman Emerson of the University of Toronto hurried out to Sheek Island in the middle of the battleground. Word had reached him that a bulldozer had turned up an unusual arrowhead. At the site, his crew unearthed knives, drills, pipes, and adzes that were 3,500 years old, matching designs retrieved in Siberia. The power commission sent Dr. Emerson their best bulldozer operator, who surprised the scientists by shaving precise three-inch layers for them.

Simultaneously, construction was underway on four other sections of the seaway. It was important that all five sections be finished together so that vessels could travel the whole length. They were all progressing rather evenly; however, east of Mercier Bridge on the Lachine section, land expropriation had not been completed. When the Canadian Seaway Authority came to buy a small Caughnawa Indian village in the path of the canal, they encountered the superintendent general of Indian affairs, whose special appraiser put a value on these lands higher than that generally paid but in line with Canadian policy toward native peoples. The Indians, under the guidance of the superintendent, took the government's offer to court. As bulldozers worked their way toward the village, the courtroom haggling stretched out, and more and more construction diesels shut down. The matter was settled satisfactorily for all the Indians except six braves, who refused to leave their dwellings even at that price.

The Seaway Authority had enough problems without the encouragement of published cartoons showing their eviction of six attractive Indians; nor could they well afford the precedent of paying these holdouts more than they had paid others. But by this time fleets of expensive machinery had ground to a halt at the borders of Caughnawaga, their expensive operators standing by.

The Seaway Authority assessed its alternatives, went to the Exchequer Court, and paid a bonus settlement to the six who had stood their ground. Even as the six Indians loaded their carts, the construction diesels cranked up.

On the eighteen-mile Beauharnois section, the canal bed and power station sites, called the Soulanges, had to be excavated almost totally through rock so hard that bulldozer blades lasted only one day. Crawler tractor pads had to be replaced every three weeks, and drillers did well to average four feet per hour.

Back on the International section, tourists driving by in June 1958 thought the natives were seeing a mirage. On the dry shore of a dry lake, the future power pool of Lake St. Lawrence, was moored a line of new rowboats. They awaited an instant lake. Workmen were mounting a new sign—"Long Sault Marina."

The climactic moment for flooding the dry lake—and completing the St. Lawrence Seaway—was at hand. Del Smythe was receiving reports throughout the night. All ships above the works and below as far as Montreal were anchored or berthed. All contractor gear was out of the cut. All inspectors were out except for two trucks racing south with sweeping spotlights, checking.

"What about those pottery diggers?"

"Who?"

"Those arrowhead guys."

"They'll be out in fifteen minutes."

At 0800, Dr. Otto Holden, Ontario Hydro's chief engineer, pressed a button. Two clouds of dirt rose from the cofferdam, throwing boulders a thousand feet into the sky. The St. Lawrence broke through two gaps and boiled northeast in a wall of water, which an hour later smashed against the Cornwall power dam.

Three days later, on July 3, 1958, about a hundred ships that had accumulated above and below the new lake began churning through the locks. The Great Lakes were officially classified by Congress as the fourth U.S. coastline.

The seven seas were now eight.

A great new trade opened immediately between the saltwater cities and Great Lakes ports.

However, not so many ships called at Cleveland. The reason for that set fourteen men into action.

7

The New Beginning, 1968–1969

Because the great potential of the St. Lawrence Seaway was not benefiting Cleveland to the extent it should, fifteen men of action selected by the mayor, Chamber of Commerce, and county commissioners met in the Tapestry Room in Cleveland City Hall at 3:00 P.M. on February 6, 1968, with an urgent mission and a twenty-four-hour deadline.

They were Harry F. Burmester, Anthony O. Calabrese, Jr., James M. Carney, Frances E. Gaul, Frederick Lynch, Jr., Thomas O. Matia, John G. Pegg, Wade E. Shurtleff, and Arthur L. Taylor. A major part of the mission was to remove the port from city and county politics. Mayor Carl B. Stokes came, as did James V. Stanton, City Council president; Edward J. Turk, chairman of Ports and Harbors Committee; and county commissioners Frank Gorman, William D. Day, and Frank R. Pokorny.

They knew that shippers in and out of Cleveland's port were frustrated in dealing with the many-layered city government, suffering delays and costs that forced cargoes to avoid Cleveland. The year the Seaway opened (1959), the Port handled under 200,000 foreign tons.

These men assembled on February 6 to create a workable port by establishing the Cleveland–Cuyahoga County Port Authority. Mayor Stokes had promised this in his campaign. Stanton pushed the bill through City Council in three weeks. The county commissioners had approved it. Councilman Anthony J. Garofoli had done the complex legal

This map by Colonel Charles Whittlesy, published in his book *Early History of Cleveland, Ohio* in 1867, is generally considered by scholars to be the most authoritative. It shows changes in the shoreline of Lake Erie and the path of the Cuyahoga River.

Arches, as shown on this cargo steamer berthed in the Cuyahoga in the early 1850s, dramatically cut down the breakup of wooden vessels in storms. Invented by shipbuilder Captain George Jones, the arches were anchored deep inside the hull to stiffen the ship and prevent it from breaking up amidships.

Boats on the Ohio and Erie Canal hauling coal and wood to Cleveland in the 1880s. The canal ran from Portsmouth on the Ohio River to Cleveland, connecting with schooners for all points. (A. C. Meakin Collection)

Early Cleveland harbor scene, date unknown. (Cleveland Press Collection/CSU Archives)

Schooners tied up on the Cuyahoga, ca. 1885. Note the two ore unloading platforms jutting out from the near bank. (A. C. Meakin Collection)

Cleveland harbor at Irish Town bend on the Cuyahoga, ca. 1880.
(A. C. Meakin Collection)

Unloading iron ore at Cleveland in 1885. Five days were often required to unload one ship. In the hold, men shoveled the ore up onto a platform. There, others shoveled it into barrels that were then winched up to a deck platform and the ore poured into wheelbarrows. A relay of men wheeled the ore onto the docks. (A. C. Meakin Collection)

Winter lay-up at Benesch's Dock, Cuyahoga River, 1880.
(A. C. Meakin Collection)

work to make this concept workable. But, on February 6, it was only a piece of paper.

By unanimous consent, Mayor Stokes assumed the acting chairmanship in this meeting and swore in the Port Board of Directors, which then elected officers: Harry Burmester, chairman of Union Commerce Bank, chairman; Jim Carney, vice chairman; John Pegg, secretary. The mayor made office space available on a one-dollar lease in one of the city's lakefront warehouses at 101 Erieside.

This Board faced immediately two uphill challenges: persuade city voters to approve transferring city port facilities to the Port Authority and persuade city and county voters to approve a tax levy to support this new Port Authority. The Board knew that, if it failed at either, there would be no Port Authority and that it must act immediately because the next day, February 7, was the deadline for putting these issues on the ballot for the May 7 election.

The Board passed Resolution 68-1, containing the rules and regulations, and it also approved the following:

a 0.13-mill tax levy to be presented to the electorate on May 7, 1968; negotiations on a five-year lease of port facilities from the City of Cleveland; formulation of a long-term development plan; the negotiation of a long-term acquisition of port facilities.

The levy, if passed, would produce about one million dollars annually for five years; expenses would be $888,000 (including a yearly lease payment to the city of $257,000). The Board predicted that this would leave a surplus for capital improvements of $220,000.

The plan and purpose of the Port Authority was now in place; a subsequent meeting would handle the other housekeeping tasks of committees and office staff.

The next meeting was set for February 17, 1968, at 9:30 A.M.

Passing the levy would be the first big task. Soon after (and in anticipation of the 0.13-mill levy being passed in May), seven of the city's bond investors offered their combined help to develop further financing plans.

Selling the First Levy

Following the mayor's and commissioners' appointment of a start-up board of directors, it was necessary to have those two pieces of legislation passed by the voters.

The first required legislation would be a 0.13-mill levy, Issue 5, for the partial support of the Port (county vote) and the second a change in the city's charter amendment, Issue 7, to enable it to lease, and/or sell, the city-owned land and docks to the Port Authority.

To grasp the challenge involved, picture selling such a levy to the bulk of taxpayers who are almost totally unaware of harbor activity and any relevance to their households. Marine activity was largely screened from their eyes by lakefront warehouses or the steep banks of the industrial valley. Even those who occasionally enjoyed a dramatic view of an ore carrier from Jim's Steakhouse hardly related marine activity to their own well-being. The docks were fenced off to spectators.

And now they were to vote to pay for this?

Evidence that the Board knew the uphill sell needed to gain passage was the very powerful group they mobilized: the Growth Association and the political bodies, the Citizens Committee for Port Authority, Port of Cleveland Information, Inc.

This group was chaired by Vernon Stouffer, Cleveland's noted restaurateur and hotel man. Directors of the group were from the International Longshoremen's Association (ILA), Growth Association, Cleveland Maritime Association, both the *Cleveland Plain Dealer* and *Cleveland Press,* all public utilities, major banks, and corporations. The group's task was to blanket the electorate with the advantages of the Port Authority mainly as an aid to businesses and as a provider of jobs.

The proceeds of the 0.13-mill tax would provide seed money for development and promotion programs that would help provide the new jobs

and business opportunities for the area. The cost to the average homeowner was estimated at seventy-eight cents annually.

Preparing for the May 7 election, this task group launched saturation coverage of the public with various fact sheets about benefits and costs. They were also competing with a menu of other levies.

Stouffer recruited a strong group of Cleveland leaders for vice chairmen of his committee. Many other groups were mustered to the support, and a speakers bureau of Port directors and other interested parties were drafted. It was a massive job of educating voters from nearly ground zero. Few citizens knew that in 1968 22,300,000 tons of various materials came into Cleveland to private and public docks. The effect of this created an influx of an estimated $82,000,000 to the area.

Wade Shurtleff, chairing the subcommittee on public relations, broadcast the advantages in small easily grasped numbers; each ton of bulk cargo handled on public docks brings in eleven dollars of new money; each ton of general cargo, twenty-five dollars.

Very active in pushing for the entire concept and the levy was James Carney, a man of several businesses, titular head of the Democratic party, a politician, and a forceful civic leader. He gave important speeches and hammered on the message that "a port is a business and it competes with other ports. It must deal with other businessmen. Under these conditions, the slow moving and cumbersome procedures of a city government are inadequate with its checks and balances and numerous safe guards to insure orderly procedure." He cited as example the building of Warehouse 32, which required twenty-three legislative acts and sixty administrative decisions to get the job done.

This kind of procedure would just not work in the competitive business world. Other Great Lakes ports did not have this problem.

In February 1968, trouble reared its political head. The Cuyahoga County Mayors and City Managers Association was upset by the way the City of Cleveland handled the Port Authority matter without consulting with other elected officials. The association's members wanted answers to several questions before they would support it. Organized labor also expressed resentment; it felt it had been given too little representation.

The Cuyahoga County mayors wanted several questions answered. Would the Port be taxed? Would the Port's functions be expanded? How had the figure for rent to the city been obtained? What about the purchase price from the city? What attempts were made by the city in recent years to develop the Port? All questions were asked and answered. The may-

ors finally were agreeable.

It seems that the most effective selling points were that "this agency is essential to the operation of a port in competition with other ports for world trade and [it is able] to operate like a business rather than a department of government handicapped by partisan politics and bureaucracy."

One group, the Cleveland Real Estate Board, objected not to the Port but to the fact that the city appointed six members of the Board and the county only three, thus giving the city appointees voting control over the bulk of the county money. The city said they felt that this disparity would be rectified, as well as paying off the $11 million of Port bonds, once the authority was in action. This appointees issue, however, would persist.

These objections worried the Port Board as the vote was to be taken in a little over two months—which meant that the Board had much work to do, and quickly.

By March other groups had joined the levy promotion team. The mayor took a more prominent role, as did the heads of the Cuyahoga County Mayors Group and the City Council's Chairman of Airports and Lakefront Development and the heads of the city's major corporations. A major utility assigned a full-time press relations manager to the levy push. The Growth Association agreed to fund the levy drive through gifts from its members. Several foundations also agreed to provide funds.

A drive was launched to bring aboard all the public watchdog agencies, such as the Citizens League, the police and firemen, labor unions, both political parties, the Catholic Church, the League of Women Voters, and the Building Owners Association. This was successful.

"Get on the Ball"

On March 14, the *Plain Dealer* published an editorial urging more action to acquaint the public with the Port's levy needs and to prod the various committees to give more effort, "Get on the Ball." By the first of April all the major bodies in the county had taken a stand for the levy and its passage.

The local papers continued editorials on the need for the Port Authority. They stressed the necessity for a port to be nonpolitical and that problems of political nature rendered the port uncompetitive. Republic Steel made direct contact with its local employees with placards at the plants and offices and urged people to go to the polls and vote regardless of how they elected to vote. By the middle of April, all promotions were in full force. There were speeches, editorials, personal contacts, bill-

boards, special work in the suburbs and the churches and clubs, and there was radio and TV advertising. Of course the media did target a couple of the Port Board's members, citing what good or bad impact they would have.

Even before the election, the Port sent George Heidish on a twenty-one-day selling tour to Europe to contact leading ship owners and export-import executives in England, Germany, Sweden, Holland, and France. Even though the *Plain Dealer* was on the team, and despite the push to sell the Port issues to voters, the newspaper scolded, "Unless there is action on the part of the people . . . selling the advantages . . . the two vital port issues are headed for defeat [on] May 7. The two port issues have been Cleveland's best kept secret." The *Plain Dealer* understood that the Port was not a dinner-table topic with the voters.

A month before the election, Captain Einar Ask, master of the Norwegian *Thor River,* tied up at Dock 20 on the Cuyahoga, first 1968 saltwater arrival. Mayor Stokes capitalized on the event and staged a public promotion for Issues 5 and 7.

At the Polls

It was no landslide, however; election-day results were 174,325 for the levy and 132,334 against. Issue 7 also passed, 76,258 to 50,406. The election committee had spent $32,562.28. A goal Cleveland business had sought for twenty years was finally accomplished. And Mayor Stokes had delivered the first of his campaign promises.

The negative vote came from mainly ethnic communities, and the biggest affirmative vote came from the suburbs and the split group from the black neighborhoods.

Open for Business

The board could begin to function as a body. However, it was nothing without funding, and the levy funds would not become available until 1969.

In the June 7, 1968, meeting the Board voted to issue tax anticipation bonds of $3,165,000 to take care of the 1969 budget, pay salaries, and ensure availability of regular operating funds in the early spring of 1969 (to avoid waiting until the fall). This would permit the hiring of an executive director and staff. The required budget was already under preparation.

Open Meetings

With the organization, the plan, and the finances in place, the Board held its meetings and public hearings in the Union Commerce Bank offices while the Erieside offices were being finished and furnished. The Board opened their meetings to the public.

James Carney recommended, and the Board approved, that an independent appraiser evaluate the city property to facilitate port negotiations.

Seventy-six men applied for the position of executive director; eight were seriously considered.

Usually this newly elected Board voted unanimously. The first difficult question came on July 3, 1968; designating a depository became mired. Three of the applicants had not included oaths with their application as required by statute. This was resolved at the next meeting; the Board selected the Cleveland Trust Company for depository of inactive funds. They were also the low bidder (4⅛ percent) for the tax anticipation note. Three other bids were received at 4 percent.

John Baker of the ILA revised the plan of operation and presented it at the October 4 meeting. All upland landowners were notified that the plan would be accessible at the county, city, and port offices.

Arthur Taylor resigned from the Board. Mayor Stokes and City Council approved for the vacancy Anthony Sapienza, leader of the Beer and Beverage Driver Union.

Elbow Room Needed

The Board felt that no growth was possible without additional land. Acquisition of the Penn Central property was proposed, including the Old Parcel Post Building and seventeen acres adjacent to Dock 24. A public hearing of the Port development plan was set for November 15, 1968. Serious negotiation was underway with the mayor and staff on terms for the lease and sale of the city property. The accounting firm Ernst & Ernst would make a further study of the Port plan.

The Penn Central objected in writing and verbally at the November 15 meeting but agreed to develop the land west of the Cuyahoga River when the Port agreed to encourage the private development of other lands. Thomas Coakley, president of Cleveland Stevedore Company, praised the Port's plan and stated that his company would cooperate. In those days, meetings lasted about ninety minutes. There were, of course, many committee meetings before the regular meeting.

"Go Ask Mary"

In the understandable complexity and confusion of start-up with new people and new issues, one grand stabilizing constant was a pleasant, long-memoried woman, Mary Sher-

man. She had worked for the City Port Control and was a walking encyclopedia about previous customers, unions, issues, personnel. And at this writing she still is that, in her position as office manager. Through the years, the answer to many questions was "Go ask Mary."

The First Season

A good way to chronicle the early main events is to roughly follow the track of the Board meetings.

The Port season closed on December 5 with tonnage approximating one million tons (683,000 the previous year). Cleveland lost some cargoes due to shortage of shed space. The executive director was to be selected as soon as the transfer date for the harbor facilities and port was set.

On December 16, 1968, the Board leased the last piece of city-owned Port property with an option to buy. Rent was $256,875 per year; the purchase price was $7 million plus interest, taxes, and bonds for Port improvements. This was a very important purchase opportunity that, regrettably, was never fulfilled.

However, as this first year of the Port Authority closed, the Board was in place, and Port facilities and the main Port plan were approved. It had been a successful business year: shipments totaling one million tons and approval of a four-year levy helped secure the Port's financial foundation. With new management of operations soon to be selected, a firm base was in place.

Year Two

The Port's second year, 1969, began with a special meeting on January 27 at which the Board named Richard L. Schultz of Brownsville, Texas, executive director. They approved compensation classes and grades for officers and employees. The day-to-day management of the Port now passed from the City Department of Port Control to the Port Authority.

The Authority now went looking for additional business. They approached federal representatives about the possibility of handling Great Lakes military cargoes. Up to this time, Milwaukee and Toledo had received a good share, but the great bulk, of course, was going to the Eastern ports.

At the first meeting of 1969, directors also noted that more export tonnage was needed. In 1959 the Port handled 186,511 total tons (65,000 export), and in 1968 1,034,000 total tons (67,000 export). Much more promotion was needed.

On February 14, 1969, TV cameras covered the meeting introducing the new executive director, Richard Schultz. Colonel Butler, who had been with the Division of Port Control, was hired as assistant director. Directors who would serve a second year included Burmester as chairman, Carney as vice chairman, and Pegg as secretary.

Seamen's Service

The Board complemented the remarkable Seamen's Service on its hospitality and service to visiting crews of foreign ships. Seamen's Service is a kind of surrogate family to visiting seamen. Members could introduce seamen to area hospitals and churches, find doctors or lawyers, help write letters, make phone calls home, or just provide a sympathetic ear. The Service is totally operated by volunteers. The uninitiated would be surprised if they saw the roll of volunteers; the corps has included many of Cleveland's highest-ranking men and women, whom you might not expect on the docks. The response from foreign seamen is sincere gratitude. They write back from foreign ports.

The Port was not yet launching an all-out marketing campaign, but on March 17 it did initiate a push to reclaim the large rubber import business previously lost due to labor problems.

The Port Board met for the first time in their new offices at 101 Erieside on April 11, 1969. The lease from the city had been signed and was now official. Carney suggested a title search be made before the Port acted on purchase as provided in the lease. That search required several months.

The Board authorized other physical property improvements, including paving and lights in sheds. Announcement of the possible razing of the old Seamen's Service building sparked discussion of a new temporary facility for them at Burke Airport pending a permanent building for them at the Port.

At the May 2 meeting, the Board discussed the need and plans for a transit shed on Dock 24. They instructed the Swindell-Dressler Company to prepare plans and specs and construction schedules. Mayor Carl Stokes and Joe Cole spoke of the advantages of a local international trade center. The minutes of the meeting read, "The mayor said that he wishes to request the Port Authority build such a structure on city land adjacent to Willard Park, a joint venture with the city and the State of Ohio. He also stated that an underground garage could be built on the site . . . simultaneously." The state decided to study the idea before proceeding.

The Board discussed renegotiating the lease with the stevedoring company, Great Lakes International, and limiting the dockage charge to encourage vessels with partial loads for Cleveland to stop at the Port instead of the usual practice of proceeding

to a full-discharge port and shipping the partial back to Cleveland overland.

On June 6 the Board instructed its executive director to study several small properties along the river that the Port had acquired in the city lease. A better use for these would be required to make them profitable.

Docks 30 and 32 had some settling problems, and the Board hired Osborne Engineering to examine and recommend a solution. The Osborne study found that no problem existed. One ship did, however, run into and damage Dock 24. The Swindell-Dressler study of the Dock 24 transit shed was questioned but eventually accepted. The chairman could now take action.

Colonel Butler resigned from the staff, and the Port's representative in Belgium resigned and was not replaced.

At the July 11 meeting, after expressions of satisfaction over the smashing success of the tenth-anniversary celebration of the Seaway, the chairman reported on his meeting with the governor; the International Trade Center was still on track although no funds were presently available. By November 7, funds for the Center were still being sought. Cleveland State University had been approached, but its response was negative; a business center might be a possibility.

More Elbow Room

Land would be an ongoing preoccupation because lakefront ownership is complex.

Litton Industries was studying a plan to develop the west side of the harbor and asked the Port to drop any claim to the area. The Board declined and so advised the Army Corps of Engineers.

On August 1 the Port moved to ask the State of Ohio to give the Port sole authority and jurisdiction over all land underlying Lake Erie along its frontage. This would mean any future requests to build or change the harbor would be subject to the Port's approval.

By September, three of the river properties were being leased. Other parcels, such as the harbor master's old office and a piece of property next to the International Milling Company, would have no marine use.

Great Lakes International proposed to use part of its lease space for overflow stadium parking, paying the Port 25 percent of collected revenues.

In November the Board leased a river parcel on Merwin Street (next to the flour mill) at $3,000 per year for five years. They also determined that the Great Lakes International lease could be canceled and renegotiated. This had been a problem since the Port Authority was formed.

At that time, the Board also discussed the lease of city property by the Cleveland Stevedore Company and decided it would be advantageous to have this lease assigned to the Port Authority with a uniform policy clause for dock openings. Under city policy, dock space had to be opened to bids.

Should Ports Be Self-Supporting?

Trustees addressed the question of whether ports should be self-supporting and determined that the majority of ports should be at least half self-supporting, while very large ports, like San Diego, New York, and Boston, should be totally self-supporting. Cleveland should work toward earning half its expenses, the other half being paid by the 0.13-mill levy.

On October 3, $2,000 was authorized for an independent engineer to review the architectural plans for the Dock 24 transit shed. By the following month the Board decided that the transit shed, phase one, would be bid in parts: foundations and utilities and offices. Phase two would be for the shed itself. Low bid on the shed was $244,967 with support columns and $331,495 for unobstructed space.

In October and November the Board tended to some housekeeping. Rules and regulations as provided for in Sections 721.04 and 4582.06 of the Ohio Revised Code had not yet been adopted and were given to a committee that would prepare them for acceptance by the Board. The directors authorized a group hospitalization plan for employees.

On December 5, Richard R. Green, director of community development, spoke on the city's proposed Great Lakes Gateway development. The plan included filling the area between the East 9th Street Pier and Dock 34 for development. The land to the south of Erieside and west of East 9th Street would be planned for offices and apartments. Green's assurance of a positive effect for the Port was taken under advisement by the Board. There had been some concern that the state's amendment to the Port Authority Act might be detrimental, but it turned out to be a clean-up and enlargement program to enable ports to operate mass transit and airports.

The directors reviewed a 1966 EDA application to finance a transit shed on Docks 24 and 32; only the latter had been approved. Schultz argued that Dock 24 needed to be included at this time, with a price tag of $6,611,597. There was further discussion that the transit shed should be bid as one bid; but two were taken.

After discussion, the directors decided to hire a port engineer only after a full screening and review of the applicants.

On the last day of 1969, the Board held a special meeting establishing rates, rules, and regulations for an agreement assigning to the Port Authority the leasehold interest of the Cleveland Stadium Company and authorizing the cancellation of the leasehold interest of Great Lakes International. Passage of this motion put the Port, for the first time, in full charge of the property and its use.

During 1969, the Port had surfaced one pier and contracted for construction of a transit shed.

For the second year the Port had been profitable.

Triple Threat

Astute Board members looking ahead knew that among their challenges for increasing business were three in particular that they must somehow overcome: the containerization revolution that was now full blown; European steamship line consortia that were forming; and stepped-up railroad competition with the Seaway.

The container vessels would soon become too big to pass through Seaway locks; hence, this trade would go to Eastern ports that were designing specialized piers and tools for handling the 20- to 40-foot-long metal boxes (very like trailer truck boxes). These containers could be carried by truck, rail, and ship. Hence, vast tonnages would travel by containers.

A steamship consortia was a combination of steamship companies cooperating to eliminate redundancy of ports and carry the same tonnage with fewer ships. They tended to force available cargoes to concentrate at fewer ports. Three of these consortia were already formed in Europe.

Compounding this competition, the railroads were reducing rates to take cargoes from the Seaway.

The Port must gear up to compete for business.

8

Learning the Ropes, 1970–1971

Ships move so slowly that it is easy to overlook the very fast shifts in world supply and demand that steer those fleets. This year's prosperity in a given port does not foretell next year's, when the fleets may be sailing the opposite direction.

At the beginning of 1970, the Board's widely respected executive director, Richard Schultz, could report success—a year of superior tonnage, the second-best totals ever; gross revenues of $30,000 more than expected; a one-to-two ratio of exports to imports. Seventy percent of all tonnage was steel.

For the first time, a Cleveland mayor would lead a trade mission to Spain, Italy, Holland, and Belgium. Accompanying Mayor Stokes would be Schultz, who was optimistic that

this would lead to even higher steel exports in the coming year.

Schultz actively promoted official recognition of the Great Lakes as the fourth seacoast not merely as regional boosterism or an advertising ploy, but because such acknowledgment would entitle Great Lakes ports to federal cargoes and subsidies.

On paper, the Port appeared sound with $720,000 in treasury bills, $2,349,500 in certificates of deposit and $27,596.45 in cash. Their escrow funds were invested in long-term, 7.5 percent U.S. Treasury notes. Operating costs were easily covered by Port income, leaving the tax dollars for capital expansion.

The Port Authority took advantage of January's closed Seaway to organize and plan the future. At the top of their strategy list in 1970 was assisting the progress of the proposed Lakefront Gateway development, which would reposition the Port as the city's front door rather than the back porch.

The cold months confronted the young organization with the real-life work-a-day problems of a port authority, especially the urgency of retaining ongoing customers while finding new business. They distributed the 1970 Port Handbook, a strong promotional tool prepared in conjunction with the Growth Association. They staged seminars for local businesses and contracted with the state for foreign sales representation.

The excitement of ships and cargoes from exotic regions seemed buried under tons of administrative paper and organizational humdrum. The new Port Authority discovered that centuries of sea traffic had developed a shoreside administrative monster.

It involved them in pay raises, provisions for vacations, sick leave and auto travel allowance, equipment maintenance, and the jungle of admiralty law. They hired three new staff members to help with the load: Peter Colarochio, John Desmond, and Ingrid Demuth. The personnel committee inherited the question of accrued vacation upon termination of employment; and all these personnel matters had to be compatible with city and county practices, the Authority being accountable to both. The directors appointed Jack Hively as assistant secretary of the Board.

By summer, the Authority had established the position of port engineer and expanded Traffic Manager John Desmond's duties to include operations and security. However, in the fall they suddenly lost a director. Francis Gaul resigned to become a city councilman. Lynch assumed Gaul's duties as head of the operations committee. Later, R. D. Peters was appointed to serve out Gaul's term.

The marine community was elated when Executive Director Schultz was elected president of the Council of Lake Erie Ports. There are fifteen ports on Lake Erie, the most active then being Buffalo, Erie, Conneaut, Ashtabula, Lorain, Fairport Harbor, Port Clinton, Toledo, Port Colborne, and Port Stanley. This recognition combined with Schultz's growing reputation were good news for the Port of Cleveland, but it also meant that Cleveland could lose Schultz.

The new Port Authority now knew that all ports confront certain common pressures, all based on the harbor's ability to load and unload ships fast and efficiently enough to suit impatient vessel captains, shippers, and receivers who are all financially hurt by delays or damage.

The traditional threats to efficient dock operations are breakdowns in equipment and labor and relations between a port and its stevedore tenants and between a port and local governments. Expansion room for operations is a problem as port cities tend to encroach on the waterfronts. The raising of tariffs is hazardous to business development in view of competition from other modes. All of these conditions affect development of new business and retention of old customers. They also make ports favorite media targets.

The very reason this Port Authority was created was to increase the harbor's share of Seaway business by anticipating and minimizing these problems and the former bureaucratic impediments to efficiency.

The directors and executives set out to foresee and forestall traditional threats with forward tactics.

For centuries the quickest way for a vessel captain to spread bad reports on a harbor has been to delay his cargo loading or discharging. When dock operations are stalled by a breakdown in equipment or stevedoring or longshoremen, the captain is counting up his still-ongoing enormous hourly costs in payroll and fees. Prompt loading or discharging is so important that if a crew member is late returning to the ship, even if on ship's business, an American intercoastal captain will cast off without him. Let him catch up at another port if he can. Therefore, Desmond put the 150-ton Buckeye Booster

crane, then Cleveland's pride and a selling point, on a schedule of preventive maintenance. He ordered standby parts, a regular inspection and lubrication schedule, and a dry run several hours before any scheduled use.

Port operations are also vulnerable to strikes from several directions beyond a port authority's control. Facing a spring truckers' strike, the Port designed a comprehensive policy that favored ships and shippers.

After the free time period, there would be certain waiving of Port charges for storage and demurrage, a charge throughout the transportation industry for any cargo overstaying the contract-specified time limit. Specifically, the Authority would extend free time for the duration of any authorized or unauthorized strike that stops all movement of cargo on the piers. There were other provisions to protect shippers and stevedore companies.

Historically also, ports are wide open to "shrinkage." Official-looking trucks can pull in, liberate several crates, exit, and quickly get lost in traffic. Sometimes dock hands feel entitled to some cargo as a gratuity. Therefore the Port began fencing Docks 28, 30, and 32 and hired private security.

Important in the Port's forward strategy was operating profitably. News of the Port's intention to raise tariffs drew increasing complaints.

Most complained that the raise would hit their businesses hard. Despite heated protests, the Port did raise fees, and in June the Port added a special tariff for barge dockage.

The raise became important. Despite the truck strike and a late Seaway opening, which reduced volume by about 75,000 tons, business for May (174,610 tons) remained favorable. However, June tonnage plunged to 97,235 tons (compared to 128,274 tons in 1969). Seaway usage also fell 17 percent.

Big demand for steel in Europe and Asia lowered steel imports. Exports from Cleveland were also down, as special government-approved rail rates for the Eastern railroads drew steel to Eastern ports.

Part of the forward strategy, with the Seaway promise in mind, was trying to buy elbow room on the shore. They were especially eager to buy land from Penn Central Railroad, which owned twenty-seven choice acres (Dock 20, the Parcel Post Building annex, and seventeen acres behind Piers 24 and 26). The politically powerful James Carney led the negotiation but regretfully reported that Penn Central was not selling. Negotiations would go on for years over this huge and famous ore and coal loading and unloading dock on prime lakefront property.

The Pennsylvania Railroad Ore Dock had been one of the wonders of World War II. Four shipside Huletts unloaded the ore boats into a steady parade of hundreds of hopper cars crawling under the Huletts from seven concentric oval railroad tracks, setting fantastic tonnage records. For example, on July 8, 1946, 970 cars were loaded with 61,530 tons of ore in just twenty-four hours. At 1946 boat capacities, that would be about six boatloads.

By the time the Port Authority was born, the great Pennsylvania Railroad was dying. Squads of attorneys tied up the Pennsylvania's properties in litigation. Striving to recover the most it could from its many properties, the Pennsylvania's rear guard held out against the Port's offers.

Hence, the Port was still on the prowl for additional land. Chief Engineer John Wolf contacted Congressman William Minshall for a third time asking his help in getting the state to give the Port a lease on all submerged land across the harbor front. Much later the Authority wrote a new lease with the State of Ohio for the underwater land. This was such an important contract that Board Director Calabrese drove the lease to Columbus to get the governor's signature.

Future Watch

The Port was still hoping for an International Trade Center and Gateway. Even more important, since the new thousand-footers could not navigate the bends in the Cuyahoga River, the Board considered alternatives. How could they make the Cuyahoga usable for the new thousand-foot vessels? At what cost? They even requested a Corps of Engineers review of the harbor that might suggest other improvements. Some ports, such as Indiana's Burns Harbor, levied use taxes to pay for construction. If the Port could not reshape the crooked river, perhaps machinery and facilities could be placed for unloading at lakeside and then sending cargo upriver to the furnaces via conveyor belts.

Looking to the future, the Port needed to become a stronger player in the containerization revolution that was sweeping marine transportation faster than the railroads went piggyback. These 20- and 40-foot containers, easily hoisted aboard, reduced longshoremen costs, reduced pilferage, and expedited schedules. The Port estimated that in 1971 it could handle 3,300 containers, three times its 1970 total. But that was still insignificant. A single ship could carry 3,300 containers. Port staff studied possibilities for special vehicles for handling more 40-foot containers.

Reality Strikes

In September, the first state audit gave the Port a clean report. However, by October management was focusing on troublesome continuing issues: the Penn Central and Parcel Post properties and the Corps of Engineers harbor parking plans. But dominating the Board's attention was a serious slowdown in imports, and it began examining new investment policies to increase Port revenues.

In any commercial harbor, there is always tension between the port and its stevedore tenants. They need each other to get the ships loaded; but they are also in each other's hands when it comes to attracting or repelling business. Sometimes the stevedore tenants overpower the landlord port authority with coercive demands; sometimes the reverse. A balance is needed or the docks become Port Chaos for shippers and ships. Agents and fleet owners find other routes. Port management deliberately launched a new initiative for the cooperation and exchange of ideas between the Authority and the powerful stevedore tenants who were on the docks before the Port Authority was born.

A port's success is also closely linked to the success and reputation of its city. It might not seem important, but fleets do like a good crew town where, on a four- or five-hour loading, seamen can get to town easily and find exciting shopping, theater, and museums and can add a famous city to their lists. Therefore, the Port worked with the Growth Association and the Lake Carriers' Association and the Lake Carriers' Association on future planning for metropolitan transportation, the proposed Jet Port, highway development, Burke Lakefront Airport, and the Corps of Engineers harbor review. Port executives were learning the pace of governments. The last Corps of Engineers review was in 1946, published eleven years later, and acted upon in 1960. This type of report was necessary to qualify for federal aid. Considering that kind of lag time, it was important to begin a new study early.

Financial Vise

With the ice coming soon, the Port's big concern was the flat general business level, especially in the Latin American countries.

Port business was down 24 percent, and profits were below expectations. Many other ports were also slow; Houston was down 20 percent and New York 15 percent. Only Baltimore showed an increase. It did not help that the State of Ohio had closed its foreign office, leaving the Port with no face-to-face sales effort abroad.

These conditions threatened the financial goal of the Port to be self-supporting (except for capital improvements). Realizing there would be good and bad times, the tariff was to be studied and raised again if possible.

Maintaining profitability could not be at the expense of ability to receive and service ships. Hence, paying large maintenance and repair costs was imperative. For example, in 1971 a heavy lift crane broke its boom, and a wayward ship extensively hammered Dock 26.

Squeezed between diminishing tonnage and resistance to increased tariffs, the Port nevertheless gingerly raised tariffs.

In retaliation, the dominant Hapag-Lloyd group of steamship lines threatened to divert their ships from Cleveland. The Japanese line, Mitsui, also raised serious objections to the increases.

The Port attempted to assure them that the net effect of the tariff changes would not materially increase their costs and worked at assuaging the anger by being extra cooperative. For example, the 1971 Seaway opening was delayed until April 14. This created some demurrage charges for shippers, which the Cleveland Port deferred.

The year 1971 opened with a $795,000 increase in equity on the Port's balance sheet; final tonnage figures for 1970 were 753,843 short tons, compared with 984,353 in 1969.

What was good or bad for the Port was good or bad for the city and vice versa. The Cleveland Stevedore Company calculated that every ton of steel across the docks brought eight dollars into the local economy and general cargo had a twenty-four-dollar impact.

The Port Handbook estimated the value of Cleveland's harbor to the Greater Cleveland economy at $200 million annually in direct benefits and perhaps as high as $2.5 billion when including value added in local manufacturing. The Port was a valuable asset to the regional economy, but how would the Port management keep it solvent?

Two bills pending in state legislature in April would help. Both would have an impact on the Port Authorities Act. Toledo Bill S.B. 122 would extend powers and duties of Port Authorities to include airports and increase the size of contracts requiring public biddings from $1,000 to $2,500. Second, the Lorain Bill S.B. 165 would increase the amount of the tax that a Port Authority may levy from .55 mill to 1.0 mill.

There was some good news for Great Lakes ports. Railroad rates had hurt them by making it attractive for Midwest shippers to use ocean ports. Rates to coastal ports were low; rates to Great Lakes ports were high. The Interstate Commerce Commission finally helped Great Lakes ports by enforcing more equal rail and truck rates to the Great Lakes ports and Eastern and Gulf Coast ports.

Another encouragement was a re-opening of the argument to lengthen the shipping season on the St. Law-rence Seaway and Great Lakes. The Merchant Marine Act of 1980 provided $9.5 million to study winter navigation and create a model. Opposition to lengthening the season came from several interest groups, especially from utilities, which claimed that ice breakers created great plates of ice that jammed their intakes.

Number-One Priority

In January 1971, Chairman Burmester cited the number-one project: enlarging the harbor and finding ways to service the huge new self-unloading ore carrier boats to earn their business. (Even though ore carriers are larger than many ships, they are still called "boats.")

To that end, Schultz and Burmester made trips to Washington to solicit support for the $9.45 million budgeted for the Cleveland harbor work and for the $10,000 to begin a review of the Cleveland harbor project.

The Authority negotiated with Penn Central for land on Whiskey Island where dockage could be built for thousand-footers. The ore might then be barged up the river or moved by railroad or conveyer belt. Extreme measures would be justified to avoid losing to other ports these thousand-footers carrying upwards of 40,000 tons but unable to navigate the crooked Cuyahoga upstream to the mills. The Corps of Engineers estimated that it would need three or four years to complete a review and determine the most practical future development of Cleveland's harbor.

However, the Port's need to capture cargoes was more immediate. As early as June 4, 1971, the marine community witnessed the christening of the *Roger Blough*, then the largest ore carrier ever built, capable of hauling nearly 50,000 tons and self-unloading 10,000 tons per hour! If the Port could not help the *Roger Blough* navigate the Cuyahoga, could it find a way to accommodate her on the lakefront?

The Authority began a close watch on the side-port loading and pre-palletization of cargo to see if that could beat containers in the cost competition.

This Port was good at handling a wide variety of other cargoes. For example, an interesting cargo went out on the *Ternefjell*, 473 walnut logs worth $2,300 each.

On May 25, 1971, the first Polish ship ever to call at Cleveland, the *Zakopane*, came to load a large bridge crane for a steel mill in Dortmund, West Germany. The cross beam for the crane was 102 feet long. A Polish sister ship picked up a second crane the following week.

Challenges from Home and Abroad

Worrying Port managers was a new threat posed by vessel owners. Shipping lines were forming consortia for making economies. Under this cooperation they would send one fully loaded vessel into the Great Lakes instead of several partially loaded.

Theft continued to be an issue. The Cleveland Stevedore Company reported theft losses in excess of $5,000; Great Lakes International said their losses topped $10,000. The situation was aggravated by reports that federal customs people were neglecting their security checks, which may have accounted for some of the thefts. The Port augmented its hired security service by employing a security supervisor.

The Port was always alert for expansion possibilities. When Cleveland's City Council passed an ordinance vacating Erieside Avenue, making it available to the Port, the Authority planned a new entrance with a guard house and fencing.

The Port sought additional space to store 60,000 tons of customers' newspaper print. While the Nicholson Terminal was sold to a group of investors for use as a paper warehouse, Bowater vessels (paper) continued to be handled through the Port Authority facilities.

In the fall of 1971, the Port applied

to the U.S. Economic Development Administration for $1,250,000 for construction of warehouse facilities. Schultz met with the Economic Development people in an attempt to expedite the grant but was disappointed with the slow-motion process.

The survey of the Penn Central property on the twenty acres behind Dock 24 south of the Erieside extension was finally complete. The Port and Penn Central Railroad agreed that 58.4 acres was the total for the property owned by Penn Central east of the Cuyahoga River. But problems continued. While the directors wanted to move ahead rapidly in acquiring this property, Penn Central remained reluctant to talk dollars.

The year 1970–71 had been a challenging boot camp for the Port Authority, and economic forecasts indicated that the future would not be easier.

9

Politics, Money, Ice, and Ships

In four years, 1972–76, the personnel of the new Port Authority became veterans in the ancient and contentious business of serving ships. Laboring between the masters of the sea and the political masters of the land, they worked at fulfilling the original purpose for creating the Authority— to capture a larger share of the Seaway trade by relieving ships of bureaucratic hurdles and creating a port so efficient as to attract shippers.

Confronting them in this were politics, financial challenge, international issues, and nature's powerful forces.

The 1972 Port year brought dramatic personnel changes, a need to prepare for the levy renewal, and the end of the ILA labor contract. Most frustrating was the need to prepare for the levy passage in the face of an outbreak of bitter confrontational politics.

After years of fairly amicable relations with all civic bodies, political hostility threatened the levy, and in fact the very existence of the Port Authority.

Also at the outset of 1972 came the retirement announcement of the fine start-up chairman, Harry F. Burmester, who had guided the Authority effectively for four years. The new mayor, Ralph J. Perk, appointed the gregarious Albert W. Bernstein, restaurateur, attorney, trustee of the National Air Races Board, and member of a roundtable of influential Clevelanders looking to the well-being of Cleveland, sans portfolio. The mayor also appointed former Republican councilman J. W. Kellog to the Board. Kellog was a lawyer long active at City Hall.

Pending seating of the new members, James Carney served as acting chairman. However, there had been a long freeze between Perk and Carney since 1962, when Perk defeated Jim Carney's brother, "Iron John," for county auditor. This coolness endured through Perk's defeat of Jim Carney for mayor and heightened when Perk appointed Bernstein chairman over Carney.

The Board had always been criticized for its total absence of marine experience. Hence, it did not help that Bernstein's opening comment to the *Cleveland Press* was, "I first took an interest in ports last year when I visited my son . . . at University of Houston. They have a fine port there."

During the Authority's four-year start-up, Board seats were not aggressively coveted. But as the Authority gained success and stature, Board membership attracted veteran politicians.

Attorney Joseph W. Bartunek, former state senator and chairman of the county Democratic Executive Committee, eyeing the expiring Board terms of Thomas Matia and James Carney, announced ambition for a Board seat. For this he had plenty of political markers to call. To accommodate him and facilitate this, his Democratic colleagues sparked a

movement to increase the Board's size to twelve members. The county commissioners had always smarted over the fact that the city made six board appointments, the county only three. This new proposal urged six and six.

The controversy awakened Estal Sparlin, a director of the Citizens League, who urged to the contrary: "*Reduce* the Board to seven and take away their $4,800 salaries. The money paid to the Board should instead be diverted to additional professional staff."

The controversy also focused media attention. A corps of reporters closely watched as Port politics developed. Especially active were James Marino, Ray DeCrane, Tony Natale, Norman Mlachak, Charles Tracy, and Julian Griffin of the *Cleveland Press* and Steve Blossom, William F. Miller, Richard D. Zimmerman, and John Clark of the *Plain Dealer*.

On February 10, 1972, the *Plain Dealer* ran the following editorial:

Keep Politics out of Port

The move to increase membership of the Port Authority is political flim-flam . . . blatant political maneuvering that should be dropped at once.

Behind this is a problem confronting Democratic party leadership. Joseph W. Bartunek . . . suddenly wants to be a member of the Port Authority. James M. Carney, unsuccessful mayoral candidate last fall, wants to be reappointed now that his term has expired. Democrats on the County Board of Commissioners don't want to dump a Democrat.

This accounts for the talk about enlarging the board.

It should be stifled.

Suddenly Republican county commissioner Seth Taft weighed in with a threat to kill the Authority: "The 1968 contract between city and county is probably void; the Port Authority has now no legal status."

He based his opinion on the strict interpretation of the enabling legislation, which he said required equalizing the city and county appointments by 1971.

This highly reported squabble segued directly into an equally public argument about Board salaries. Reporters studied other port boards and publicized the fact that the average board salary in sixty-seven other ports was forty dollars per monthly meeting, while Cleveland directors received $4,800 a year for twelve meetings.

The attack on Board salaries came even from friends of the Port. For example, Ray W. Luzar, president of the Ohio Foreign Commerce Association, pointed out that New York and Houston directors received no salaries. "We've been double crossed," he told the media. "Shippers en-

dorsed the formation of an Authority . . . now the directors are abusing it."

Extending into March, this argument was damaging to the new levy campaign underway for the November election. Foster & Kleiser Company donated twelve prime billboards. An impressive ship silhouette loomed over the traffic and the slogan "Port of Cleveland—Gateway to World Markets."

On March 23, 1972, the county commissioners granted Joseph Bartunek his sought-after appointment to the Board and reappointed Jim Carney. In making the appointments, the commissioners urged the Board members to give up their salaries. Republican Seth Taft charged, "A just retired Democratic chairman has just been appointed to the Port Authority by his successor party chairman. This is bad government. Call it the 'retiring chairman's award.'" Taft said he had respect for Bartunek, "But special qualification for the Port, *he does not have*." Thomas Matia, who was not reappointed, termed the Bartunek appointment "a political pay-off." There were threats of lawsuits.

Richard Schultz declared to *Plain Dealer* reporter William Miller that "the last thing the Authority needs is a court case. There are more productive things to be done here."

This 1972 politics continued to threaten right on into 1975. County

Commissioner Seth Taft, credited in political circles for sincerity, said he would work to defeat a $22-million Port levy to buy the city Port property unless the Board appointment ratio between city and county were reversed to six county appointees and three city. Taft claimed, "As with other services, Cleveland doesn't want to lose control. It just wants someone else to carry the deficit."

Authority chairman Albert Bernstein, a city appointee, said, "There is no chance the ratio will be changed."

Finance and Operations

Amid continuing political distractions, Port operations advanced the mission of acquiring more of the Seaway business.

There had been a rising push for a longer shipping season, one manifestation of that was that two ore boats, the *Voorhees* and the *Fairless,* ran until February 5, 1972. While this iron ore trade had no bearing on the Port's business, it encouraged the hope for a longer season and expanded business for every Great Lakes port.

A major limiting factor for Cleveland continued to be a shortage of space. Cleveland lost tonnage to other ports because it did not have enough space to serve all types of cargoes. Therefore, the Authority was land hungry.

Occasionally there was progress

on this front. Jim Carney's frustrating negotiations with Penn Central finally matured with a firm agreement for purchase of 17.9 acres south of Dock 24 for about $2 million with an option on an additional seven acres. The Port also acquired the lease of 6,293 acres of underwater land.

In addition, the Port officers needed to see that operations on neighboring lands did not damage the harbor's chances for expanded shipping. For example, rising throughout 1972 was enthusiasm about a jetport to be built out in Lake Erie, connected to the lakefront by a causeway. The Port, as authority over all land under the water on the Cleveland lakefront, needed to monitor this to safeguard shipping operations.

Warehouse space was also sorely inadequate. Economic Development Administration (EDA) funds for the 60,000-square-foot warehouse came through for $1.25 million. The balance of the cost, $3,896,000, would be paid by the Port.

Prospects looked good for the oncoming general cargo season, perhaps a third million-ton year. Thirty-three upbound vessels were waiting in the Montreal area for the ice breakers. However, Managing Director Schultz worried that "the Longshoremen's contract comes up at the end of March. This year there may be a problem because New York is behind in settling." A guaranteed annual wage was one of ILA's goals, which could be tough. Discussions began in Cleveland on April 7 just days before the season was to open.

The first arrival of the 1972 season, the French *Eglantine,* with 10,600 tons of steel coils from Holland, tied up at sundown on April 18.

A very interesting ship, *Ocean Endurance,* arrived. Although flying the Pakistan flag, she was something of a ship without a country because of the civil war between East and West Pakistan. She was built originally to ferry passengers between those two halves. Since the civil war, however, the *Endurance* roamed foreign trade routes bringing steel from Japan, hauling grain from Lake Superior to Britain, and carrying steel back to Cleveland from Europe.

A dramatic export in May was a complete steel mill for Argentina's Somisa Steel Company. The large number of huge components, built in Alliance, Ohio, required three vessels and the Port's 150-ton Buckeye Booster crane.

Other especially large export shipments came from Cyril Bath Company of Solon, Ohio, including parts for huge presses bound for England, and from Bardons & Oliver, large lathes for Algeria.

The 525-foot Indian *Jalarajin* tied up just long enough to load eighty-eight tons of machinery for Bombay, a 12,000-mile haul. Instead of the usual thirty- to thirty-five-man crew,

this ship carried sixty-five. Captain Stone explained that Indian ships often have three galleys requiring additional cooks to prepare special religious diets for Hindu, Moslem, and other religions.

A very big day came in June, when nine overseas ships (from Sweden, Canada, Germany, Japan, Holland, and Italy) filled all but two berths.

On the stormy night of June 22, two ocean freighters rocked by eight-foot waves smashed repeatedly against the Port piers. At Berth 30, the Polish vessel *Zakopane* tore the timber bumpers off the pier and smashed the steel-reinforced concrete and also damaged itself. At Berth 28 the Norwegian *Utvik* cracked the pier wall. The ships were crashing with such force that the Port offices shook.

In July the unusual Norwegian *Sneland* brought a load of Dutch coiled steel. Touring this new ship was an experience. There was no ship's wheel on the bridge, merely a control panel of buttons and lights and a lever like a stick shift. The two 6,000-horsepower engines could be switched onto computer monitoring or operated from the bridge. Crew quarters and recreation areas were deluxe, even including a swimming pool.

The largest export through the Port thus far was from the General Motors Terex plant in Hudson: fourteen huge earthmovers. They loaded onto the *Amazonia* on August 9, 1972, headed for Rio de Janeiro to build highways.

Later, thirteen 105-ton off-highway Euclid mining trucks loaded out of the Port for the copper mines in New Guinea. The total sales price was $4.6 million, radios included.

Arriving from France that fall was a beautiful, exact replica of the Liberty Bell consigned to the Liberty Garden in Canton, Ohio. "Many children will never get to historic Philadelphia, so we're bringing it to them," explained one of the garden's founders, Richard Smart.

In October, the Port shipped a 27,000-pound crate to Taiwan. Inside was a 400-degree furnace for making aluminum cans.

In November the Werner G. Smith Company pumped 160 tank-truck loads of linseed oil into the tank vessel *Stolt-Atlantic*. That oil, 7.8 million pounds of it, was the largest linseed oil shipment out of the Port. It was headed for paint manufacters.

Returning from the trade mission to Moscow, Odessa, Murmansk, and Leningrad, an optimistic Chairman Bernstein reported that at least six Russian ships would dock in Cleveland by July. However, the mission's good progress was later grounded by a government sandbar.

Organizing for a critical 1972 levy campaign, the Board put Richard Peters and government liaison Sapienza on the public relations committee. Carney chaired the finance committee. Ohio Bell Telephone lent public relations specialist Herb Hackenbury to help with levy promotion.

The levy would need serious help as possible opposition emerged from several powerful quarters. For example, the possible future jetport in Lake Erie gathered momentum. Republican county commissioner Seth Taft carried into summer his charge that the Port Authority did not exist. Accordingly, the future jetport would not be considered part of the Port Authority. He stated that the county would probably not support the Port levy.

The Port Board countered by explaining the many functions of the Authority and its importance to the operation of a successful port.

Former opponents began to switch their influence to levy passage. In October, newspapers, labor unions, and both political parties endorsed the levy.

The Cleveland Maritime Association, long a proponent for returning the Port to city control, reversed its position less than a month before the election, but it continued to object to the Board's lack of maritime personnel.

Despite the severe political infighting and hostile publicity, the levy passed by a very strong margin (77,681).

Great Expectations

Nineteen seventy-three opened with a rainbow of enthusiasms arching Cleveland's skyline—the proposed Lakefront Gateway Development; the new 9th Street pier; a proposed World Trade Center, a new lakefront development to be seeded with $17 million from the Higbee Company; the lagging Corps of Engineers harbor study received a kick restart by Ohio congressmen; and the jetport idea stayed alive. Especially invigorating was the prospect of attracting Russian business to the Port.

Would these dreams come true?

James Carney offered to travel to Russia at his own expense to sell Russians on using the Cleveland–Cuyahoga Port. The Port, however, decided on an official plan for a trade mission. James Carney would visit four Russian cities from February 1 to March 22.

Mayor Perk and the county commissioners worked under pressure to appoint Board members with marine knowledge, but more time would pass before this would happen. The mayor appointed John J. Felice, Jr., to replace Richard Peters. Felice was secretary-treasurer of Teamsters Local 293, where his father served as president.

The Russians

Whatever other dreams might stag-ger, on the afternoon of April 25, a Soviet ship sailed along Cleveland's east shore and slipped into Dock 32 north at 4:10 P.M. to unload seventy-five tons of Russian plate glass. There were no bands playing. Security was tightened lest there be any anti-Soviet demonstrations. A few officials from the Authority came to watch the docking of the *Stanislavsky*, which flew the hammer and sickle. She had come from Murmansk on the Arctic Circle.

The Seamen's Service offered thirty-five free tickets for the crew to attend the Great Moscow Circus at the Arena, but the men were too tired to attend. They had spent the previous night working the *Stanislavsky* through the Welland. The ship, a year older than its forty-one-year-old Captain Nazarov, was in good condition.

As the ship was about to cast off, Captain Nazarov called down to the departing Cleveland guests: "If you see the mayor, tell him I like Cleveland okay!"

In July the Russian *Angarges* arrived with machinery and special ore.

In November the Russian *Donetsky Khimik* arrived to pick up one hundred huge crates of industrial rubber processing equipment for Murmansk from International Basic Economy Corporation (IBEC) in Strongsville.

Russian ships carried 6,000 tons out of Cleveland. There were hopes of tripling that in 1974.

But near the end of 1973, Soviet trade was threatened unless trade agreements with Russia could be revised. Noel Painchaud, president of Great Lakes International Corporation, explained that the U.S. Export/Import Bank and Maritime Administration specified that 50 percent of American-made goods purchased by foreign nations must be shipped in vessels of the U.S. Merchant Marine fleet. However, there were no international U.S. ships operating in the Great Lakes.

Until September 30, Russians had a waiver of the 50 percent regulation and could carry unlimited U.S. export cargo in their own ships.

Security

Pilferage at the Port was down from the 1971 high of $175,000. Director Schultz, chairman of the Risks and Insurance Committee of the American Association of Port Authorities, noted that "The Port of Cleveland is held up as a good example of security when government agencies compare ports."

But pilferage lingered. A security study noted that unauthorized access to the port was too easy. Their men were able to enter the Port by land and by water unchallenged. Among their recommendations was the moving of the union hiring hall and employee parking to outside a fenced dock area. Chauncey Baker, head of Local 1317 welcomed the suggestion, "because I think longshoremen get blamed for a lot they don't do." He noted that missing items could be stolen by truck drivers and by personnel at a ship's previous ports of call.

While security recommendations were gradually implemented, some, like creating the Port's own police force, were too expensive.

Pursuing Business

The containerization revolution, with its many advantages, accelerated in coastal ports to the east, south, and west of Cleveland. It remained attractive for shippers to railroad cargo across the country to ocean ports because containers were relatively theft-proof, rail rates for containers stayed low, and loading/unloading was simpler and thus cheaper.

In an effort to help stevedore companies expand into the container business, a committee was formed to examine options. This committee consisted of two board directors, a stevedore company executive, and an ILA officer. Increasing container business would require more dock space, more specialized equipment, and big investment. Even if all that were acquired, the bottleneck that local ports could not break was downstream—the outdated Welland Canal was too narrow to handle the wide-bodied container ships capable of stacking 3,000 boxes on deck.

Crash Marketing

Port tonnage for 1973 was down 23 percent due largely to the business boom in Europe and devaluation of the U.S. dollar. Alarmed by the low activity on the docks, the Authority launched another crash development program. All Great Lakes ports were suffering declines, but Cleveland set out to contact all Port users to see if they could forecast next year's shipping. The new development plan called for stepped-up promotion and trade missions.

The year ended with the city and the Port deadlocked on terms to renew their expiring lease. The mayor wanted to raise the rent.

The last foreign ship of the season cleared December 13, the Brazilian *Netuno,* its third call of 1973. Captain Edwardo Schuriz watched loading of the Euclid off-highway earthmovers onto his ship and sailed for the Welland to get to saltwater before the Seaway closed for the winter. Only thirty other foreign ships were left in the Great Lakes, all of them closer to the Welland.

Despite Cleveland's lower tonnage, 1973 was the Seaway's biggest year: over 55 million tons.

Great, bold marine dreams had opened 1973, but none broke ground except the one that the Port Author-ity initiated—the Russians had come.

Government on the Waterfront

Every large port authority lives in a complex multigovernment polity. To maintain good ship loading, unloading, and servicing operations, a port authority needs shrewd care and handling of this ever-changing political power net. A port is usually a tenant of the city and/or county; in turn, it is landlord to powerful tenants— the stevedore companies, longshoremen headquarters, and other port services. The Authority's friends on one occasion become its adversaries on another.

Cleveland's Port Authority was only different in that it had a mere half-decade's experience at learning these ropes. But even that short experience would be put to use in the next three eventful years, 1974 through 1976, during which time land, politics, financing, and weather would challenge the Port.

The Authority was now becoming experienced in seaport legal complications, and 1974 brought a tangle of them. The long, frustrating acquisition negotiations for the Penn Central property seemed settled. The Authority had taken possession and was planning to build two structures on it. Suddenly, County Auditor George Voinovich dropped a small bomb: Penn Central owed the county $243,000 in delinquent property taxes. The lawyers danced back and forth, but Voinovich said, "There will be no clear title until the county gets $243,000."

Legally, the Authority also needed to master the new Water Resources Act to get a pro-rata waiver of local cost share for dredging spoil containment dikes.

The legally unsettled carry-over lease negotiation with the city also needed to be resolved. To remain legal after the expiration of the lease, the Port paid the city the established rate of $256,875 per year. However, the city was pushing for a large raise. Negotiation was difficult, as the directors could not forecast the outcome of their new, upcoming levy campaign. If the levy was approved, the Port hoped to buy the land for $15 million.

People

The urgent chores had to be carried on smoothly despite a period of active musical chairs. Valued Board member Wade E. Shurtleff died, and the outstanding port director, Richard Schultz, resigned to head the American Association of Port Authorities, a considerable step up in stature and pay. "Losing him is a real blow," Chairman Bernstein told the media. "He deserves the job."

Emplacing a new Port director necessitated a special meeting in which the Board designated Jack Hively to replace Schultz. It also established wages, salaries, and job descriptions. However, at this same meeting, though not previously announced to Board members, the city lease was presented, even though James Carney was absent. The lease terms were $300,000 in 1974, $350,000 in 1975, and $388,000 in 1976. County Commissioner Taft voiced fears that the Board would approve the lease before equalizing city and county Board representation. And it did just that.

This led to heated discussion in the June 7 Board meeting between Chairman Bernstein and James Carney. Carney and others objected, stating that the June 3 meeting should have been *only* for electing a new or acting executive director and the lease was considered without advance copies for study. Bartunek had abstained from the vote on those grounds.

At the beginning of the year the Board was down to seven directors: Bernstein, chairman; Calabrese, vice chairman; John Felice, secretary. Vice Chairman John Kellog had resigned to become legal counsel for the Transit System.

Two Marine Men

Mayor Perk appointed two new directors: Jay Ehle of Cleveland Builders Supply (CBS), headquartered on the Cuyahoga and a large user of Lake shipping and supplier of materials for major construction projects in the Midwest, including concrete for the Eisenhower Lock at the Soo; and Loran F. Hammett, head of the largest bulk carrier fleet, U.S. Steel's Pittsburgh Steamship (his office window overlooked the docks and the marine traffic).

Thus, for the first time the Board seated two men with work-a-day experience with water commerce, docks, warehouses, stevedore companies, and maritime unions. Both these new directors were direct, laconic, confident realists.

Also appointed to the Board was Robert T. Bennett, the thirty-four-year-old vice chairman of the county's Republican Executive Committee.

In June the Board appointed Peter Colarochio as executive director at $25,000. Colarochio had solid previous experience at three ports. The following month, the Board hired Thomas J. Harmody as trade development manager.

The Business Weather

While world trade was brisk, three adverse conditions worked against Cleveland's port. The first was the closing of the Seaway in winter. Shippers naturally tended to stay with their coastal winter ports through the summer. The second factor, the federal requirement under the Cargo Preference Act to use a very high percentage of U.S. ships for export of military or foreign aid cargoes, was a trade killer. The third limitation continued to be the Welland bottleneck. Only 450 ships in the world could squeeze through, and many of them were committed to other trades.

In June 1974, Peter Colarochio declared the Port to be in a life or death struggle. "U.S. and Canadian bureaucracies are out to kill off the nation's fourth coast." He told the Board that while the U.S. Maritime Administration refuses to send American ships into the Great Lakes, it continues to insist that Cleveland load 40 percent of Russia-bound exports on American overseas ships, 40 percent on Russian ships, and 20 percent on any other flags. Even though Colarochio spent six months, including trips to Moscow, soliciting Russian business, this regulation was being enforced. Thus, business generated by Cleveland was forced to East and Gulf Coast ports. "Those ports have high priced lobbyists in Washington to push their causes. They'd like to run us out of business."

Dockside Action

Great Lakes ports struggled to maintain status quo. Except for the limiting factors cited earlier, the prospects for the next three years looked good. To the surprise of many, the State of

Ohio ranked second in the nation in export value, $2.7 billion. Ohio established a European trade office in prosperous Germany, and the Authority planned another trade mission to Europe.

Of no particular benefit to the Port, but certainly a dramatic attraction, was the refueling stop of the new 858-foot *Roger Blough* on January 31, 1974. The *Plain Dealer* ran large photos and stories about the Port's largest call ever. The *Blough* tied up at three docks, the bow on the eastern edge of Dock 26 the stern at the western edge of 24. Her late-January visit prompted Captain Neil Rolfson, Jr., to remark, "The *Blough* is either the latest vessel ever to call at Cleveland, or the earliest!"

Optimists began to believe that the Seaway shipping season was lengthening.

In 1974, under exceptionally light ice conditions, the Seaway opened on March 22, the earliest in fifteen years. When Seaway closing dates were announced, beginning with the Canadian Soo on December 12, 1974, the American Soo declared it would remain open in an experiment to test feasibility of year-round traffic. The U.S. Army Corps of Engineers received reports from steamship companies intending to operate well into February 1975.

The first foreign ship of 1974 was Odessa's *Donetsky Metallurg,* which docked on April 13. The affable Captain Ivan Bebel spoke fluent English, learned in India.

Crossing the docks in May were huge shipments of scotch from Canada, four-high stacked pallets of rope and twine from England, fluospar from Spain, coils of special steels from all over—unfortunately more imports than exports. (Not widely understood is that even at this writing some steel is imported by American steel companies.) Outbound cargo again included a shipload of walnut logs, this time bound for LeHavre, France, for fine furniture. Barreled olives coming in from the Mediterranean could not be stacked because each barrel had a five-gallon glass bottle feeding in preservatives like a hospital IV.

The British *Ajax* docked in a heavy fog and discharged 121 Volvos worth over a half-million dollars. Volvo was experimenting with using Cleveland as a distribution center. Volvo distribution manager, William Owens, was impressed with the Port: "The unloading was efficient and . . . all kinds of cooperation." The cars were unloaded in the experimental "lift on, lift off" method using a large net.

The largest overseas shipment ever to go through the Port was loaded on June 5, 1974—a vast shipment of machinery from General Tire headed for Constanza, Romania. The first of three shipments went out on the Soviet *Donetsky Shakter* of the Black Sea Line. These exports, when assembled in Romania, would become a complete factory for automotive tires. A sister ship, *Donetsky Khimik,* moored nearby, was discharging chemicals and loading rags.

Despite the demand for Port services, by July the Port's tonnage was down 37 percent. Even so, it was better off than Chicago and Milwaukee, where tonnage fell over 60 percent. According to Peter Colarochio, "The reason is an acute shortage of ships. Cleveland would be having its best year if we could get ships." Colarochio cited 166,000 tons of local cargo rerouted through Eastern ports for lack of ships, a loss of $145,000 to the Cleveland Port.

Business was further interrupted by an accident at the Welland on August 25. The *Steelton,* a Bethlehem Steel ore boat, was headed downstream, Buffalo to Quebec, when she struck the bridge five miles above the Welland. The bridge extended 120 feet above the water; its two concrete counterweights each weighed 300 tons. The collision threw one counterweight tearing into the highway; the other disappeared into the canal. Tons of rubble blocked ship traffic. Repair costs were estimated in the millions, but that would be small compared to the price tag generated by a long interruption of commerce.

Two weeks passed before a path was cleared. Just as shipping was to resume, a strike by the Canadian Pilot's Association threatened to make matters even worse.

Gilbert Navy, dock boss at Cleveland Stevedore, requested special consideration for ships seeking refuge during the pilot's strike—free dockage. The Stevedore Company also asked to have ships dock over nonworking weekends without charge.

However, the strike settled seven days later.

Cleveland berths suddenly filled and stevedore companies worked around the clock servicing ships from Greece, England, Russia, Norway, Poland, and Germany.

These two major events cut almost a month out of the 1974 shipping season, a devastating blow to the Port and to Cleveland's port-related industries.

The lost time prevented anticipated turn-around traffic. Colarochio explained, "Some would have been able to return to home ports for one more cargo destined for Cleveland before the season ends. [Now] there may not be time."

Peter Colarochio charged ahead, dedicated to advancing Port prospects despite any adversity. But on October 9, less than two weeks after Port activity had finally revived, he suffered a fatal heart attack while working in his office. At forty-six he was only in midstride. He was known and respected around the Great Lakes ports; the marine population truly mourned his loss.

Jack Hively became acting director. In March of the following year, the Port named Noel Painchaud executive director. For the first time, local television stations covered the event, possibly because Painchaud was a handsome, glamorous veteran of political posts around Cleveland. His office would be decorated not with many pictures of ships but with personal trophies, such as skydiving batons. He left the post abruptly in June 1978. Chris Howley was named to the newly created position of director of operations; Jack Hively was named deputy director for administration.

Work Continues

The desire to increase container business was still gnawing, and opinions about the possibility clashed. Conrad Everhard, president of Dart Containerline, told Cleveland import-export executives at the Athletic Club to "forget it, you'll never get it."

The Great Lakes Commission remained optimistic.

The container revolution in ocean coastal ports came about so quickly because of the tremendous benefits to nearly all parties. The containers could be loaded and sealed right at the shipper's factory and then moved by rail or truck flatbeds directly to shipside. A rectangular crane fixture drops to the box and hooks onto four rugged grips on the top four corners

of the container. The crane hoists the box onto the deck or into the hold. Containers stack so high on the deck that a layman wonders why the ships don't capsize in a strong wind. Off-loading at the destination port is equally facilitated by containerization.

Biggest Warehouse on the Great Lakes

In an effort to prepare the Port for its share of this growing business, construction started on a 144,000-square-foot warehouse on Port docks at Erieside Avenue. Mayor Perk and Port officials christened the structure on May 19, 1975, and announced plans to lease the space to an operator for development as a container loading and unloading facility. Construction was completed in October.

Other Moves

The longshoremen's union leased the former harbormaster property.

When the Coast Guard station on Whiskey Island at the mouth of the Cuyahoga was abandoned in 1974, more prospects for expansion opened. Jay Ehle was assigned to check into the physical plant and report any possible problems.

The Seamen's Service needed quarters closer to the Port. The Authority cooperated and found them space in the building on the East 9th

Street Pier that was dominated by the famous Captain Frank's Restaurant. In May an icy coexistence on this pier cracked. Captain Frank's Restaurant, owned and operated by short-fused Frank Visconti, was the better known of the duo leasing space on the city's pier. Also in residence were the offices of the Seamen's Service and its president, Livingston H. Ulf.

A fire in the restaurant affected both tenants, but not as dramatically as the hole punched through the wall by Visconti. He claimed that he needed space to store fire-damaged equipment and was entitled to requisition the Seamen's office because Service officials owed him money for their share of utilities and taxes. Once in, Visconti barricaded Seamen's re-entry.

A war of words stretched throughout the summer until August 17, 1974, when the husky former city port director, W. Kiely Cronin, and several Seamen's volunteers forced open a door and presented Visconti with an eviction notice.

Not intimidated, the seventy-four-year-old Visconti ripped up the note and threatened to throw them all into the lake! The Seamen's maneuver was futile, as the argument had been legally settled hours before when the Northern Ohio Community Development Corporation (NORCOM) signed a lease with the city for the entire pier. Terms of the lease required termination of all previous agreements for the pier, including Visconti's and Seamen's.

Meanwhile, NORCOM sublet the entire pier space to Visconti and offered Seamen's space in the future Gateway. Case closed!

Plans for more permanent housing for the good hearted Seamen's Service surfaced in 1975 in space just north of Municipal Stadium. Contributions built a modern office with a highly visible sign. The Service could settle down in a place foreign seamen could easily find.

Seamen's Service

Despite only cursory acknowledgment by the marine community, these 250 volunteers, many multilingual, diligently meet 200 to 300 foreign vessels annually, helping visiting seamen. Beyond the normal services, they supply the unusual. One Japanese crew wanted to see Niagara Falls and get back to their ship on time. The Service arranged a fast round trip charter to the Falls guided by volunteers. Surprising to many, the Center operates a thriving stamp-trading activity as foreign sailors bring stamps to trade.

Founder Clair McMurray Howard reported the foreign crew response as being overwhelming. They write back, they bring presents. A Greek ship captain said, "In every other country, greedy people come aboard to take our money or sell us their religion. In Russia they give us propaganda. But you just make us welcome."

Having its eye on additional Penn Central property adjacent to the Port, the Board purchased 7.55 acres for $979,793. A special committee studied the new parcel for possible public parking.

As the rent to the city for the whole Port area came due, the Board signed a lease-purchase agreement contingent upon passage of the levy. The city's asking price had climbed from $15 million to $22.5 million. The Port Authority agreed to the price if all approvals could be secured. That would prove difficult.

Rainbow of Dreams

Something in the air, probably politics, made 1975 a year for more waterfront dreams. A $67-million plan from Governor John Gilligan's outgoing administration proposed to add 150 acres to the 117-acre Gordon Park, using dredge spoil from the harbor. The state's natural resources director, William Nye, believed he could get federal funding. For lack of funding, Gordon Park had become an eyesore.

June Kosick and Hazel Seltzer, who had shepherded construction of the Cleveland Heritage Park on Merwin Avenue near the Moses Cleveland landing site, now proposed that a lake museum be put in the abandoned Coast Guard station. As others came aboard, the concept grew into an extended plan for lakefront shops and condominiums proposed by NORCOM.

On top of all this, incoming governor James Rhodes proposed a multimillion-dollar funding of Cleveland Port improvements, including a World Trade Center.

Mayor Perk had long entertained dreams of a World Trade Center in Cleveland. Perk put his vision in the hands of Nicholas A. Bucur, a veteran of numerous local commissions and boards. Plans started with a fifteen-man board of governors to be expanded later to forty-five and sixty members. Artists' concepts of a twenty-two-story World Trade Building began appearing in the Cleveland press.

Additional optimism came from the Army Corps of Engineers announcement that its long-awaited study of possible harbor improvements would be finished by June 1976. It would call for $211 million in improvements, including a conveyer belt to move iron ore and stone up the Cuyahoga to the steel mills.

There were smaller dreams, too. Jerry Powell refitted the *Flying Cloud* schooner as a floating restaurant. He brought her from Virginia, converted her to a 150-seat restaurant, and moored her in the mouth of the Cuyahoga. On a larger scale, Charles R.

Cimasi planned to bring a large-stern wheeler showboat to the lakefront. The huge vessel contained four dining rooms, two night clubs, six bars, a dinner theater, and an outdoor cafe.

Campbell Elliott, president of the Greater Cleveland Growth Association, made an elaborate proposal to the federal government for locating in Cleveland a regional office of the U.S. Maritime Administration. Cleveland was competing with Chicago and Detroit.

Law and Finance, Care and Handling

Much of any port's work is navigating the legal-financial crosscurrents. In April 1975 the Authority studied the question—did the Port have the proper legal position to issue tax anticipation bonds of $2,500,000? By June they decided to issue the bonds.

While the Authority considered the best uses for the Coast Guard building, several city department heads decided that the station would be a good home for their departments. When the Authority brought up the subject of rent, the city seemed wounded. "After all, you got it for nothing."

With one exporter the city entered a lively discussion about dockage charges, the issue being exactly when the meter starts and stops on a ship coming into port.

Meanwhile . . . the Main Business

Earlier than any other foreign ship into Cleveland since the Seaway opened, the Yugoslav *Split* sailed in through cold winds the morning of April 6, 1975. She had been buffeted against the Welland Canal locks, giving and receiving some damage. The *Split* was commanded by Captain Milan Zec, a veteran foreign trader. For example, en route to Cleveland the *Split* had stopped at Barcelona, Cadiz, Lisbon, Montreal, and Toronto; she would continue on to Detroit, Chicago, and Milwaukee. At Cleveland, the *Split* delivered 3,600 cases of wine, forty-five cartons of cork, and two drums of oil.

The Port had a low tonnage start in 1975, down about 80 percent. The low volume worsened with a strike of 2,400 dock workers in Montreal, Quebec City, and Three Rivers that delayed vessels. Nearly all ocean ships arrived at the Seaway too deeply loaded to enter. They stopped at Montreal to discharge some cargo.

The beautiful Russian *Volkhovges*, with its graceful shear, tied up at Dock 28 with a load of aluminum ingots. The forty-nine crew members were not allowed to debark because the captain would not allow Immigration to ask them if they were voluntary members of the Communist party. Captain D. Patterson of Nordship, agent for the *Volkhovges*, said, "the question by an overzealous inspector was totally unnecessary."

The Seamen's Service tried to help, but the Immigration people answered questions by citing regulations. After the Authority's efforts to solicit Russian business, this was an embarrassment.

April brought good news. Lykes Brothers Steamship Company, operator of forty-one ocean ships, established a monthly service between Great Lakes and Mediterranean–Black Sea ports. It was the first regular American liner service in the Great Lakes since 1968, when Export-Isbransdten Lines withdrew. The first Lykes vessel to arrive was the *Jean Lykes* in July, a container and break bulk ship.

In the fall a second U.S. ship company, Farrell Lines, inaugurated Great Lakes service. Their 572-foot *African Sun,* the largest ship ever through the Welland at that time, linked Cleveland to African ports at Monrovia, Abidjan, Matuch, Durban, Moubasa Beira, and Capetown. Monthly trade began with an import cargo of 1,074 tons of crude antimony oxide for Chemetron Corp's chemical processing plant in Cleveland.

In 1975, the St. Lawrence Seaway Development Corporation announced the latest closing dates thus far: no downbound ship would be accepted at the Iroquois Lock after 8:00 A.M. on December 18.

On December 13 the German *Tilly Ross* hastened cargo discharge at Cleveland to get out of the Lakes before that deadline. The fact that she hauled imports *to* Cleveland, not exports *from* Cleveland, dramatized a problem. When the *Tilly Ross* hauled east, she left behind Great Lakes ports way down in tonnage for 1975.

The Rainbow?

Dreams were fading.

The city drove off Jeffrey Powell's restaurant boat as not meeting code. The floating showboat did not come. The lake museum and the shops and lakefront condominiums faded away.

"World Trade Week" had great potential for usefulness but instead came off as a thinly veiled reelection campaign device.

The World Trade Center's board of governors was comprised of forty-five important names. However, beyond a double handful of hands-on marine men and foreign traders, the list was heavy in academics, media, and political personalities. The World Trade Center was basically a piece of paper, a list of names.

On the good side of the rainbow, the Maritime Administration office (MarAd) *did* arrive in Cleveland, headed by George Ryan. And two U.S. carriers began service to the Great Lakes, a prize at the top of the Port's wish list.

Those two victories were enough to sustain the hard corps of real maritimers in Cleveland who knew the power of a port and firmed resolve to make this port great despite winter ice, federal impediments, squabbling politicians, and dilettante dreamers.

Every successful port has a few.

Back to Basics

The 1975 season had handled more ships but 29 percent less tonnage. Chairman Bernstein organized a group to accompany the Ohio European trade mission in the spring. Port director Painchaud, trade development manager Harmody, and Chairman Bernstein were to go, and Tom Harmody would split off and go to Russia.

Beyond increasing incoming cargoes, Cleveland launched a push for *outgoing* tonnage. Henry T. King, chairman of the Ohio District Export Council and corporate international counsel for TRW and former prosecutor at Nuremberg war crime trials, led a campaign to get smaller manufacturers into exporting.

Looking long-range for increased tonnage, Port people pushed the federal winter navigation study. This $9-million federal demonstration program had completed its study on the upper Lakes and on the feasibility of keeping open the narrows between Lakes Superior and Huron. But the program was waiting for funding to work on the St. Lawrence section of the inland waterway. It also needed permission to lay a full-scale test ice boom across the river near the source of the St. Lawrence at Ogdensburg or at Galloo Island. The ice boom was to prevent huge chunks of ice broken off by ships from blocking hydroelectric water intakes. Maritime people seriously envisioned prospects for lengthening the season to January 31, or even February 15. Previously, sailing beyond November 15 was discouraged.

However, countering these moves to increase Cleveland tonnage were some threatening undercurrents. Canada began negotiations with Washington about nearly doubling the Welland Canal toll. A heavily laden vessel traversing the Seaway might pay $15,000 in tolls and lockage fees. Raising that substantially could send many more inbound ships to New York and Baltimore.

Additionally, Councilman Michael Climaco discovered that, by a Supreme Court decision, the City of Cleveland could tax imports on top of federal tariffs. Although long-sighted councilmen and city officials pointed out the disincentive to foreign shippers, Climaco's rebuttal was, "The tax could keep out cheap foreign goods which now compete unfairly with American-made goods." There was no action on this in 1975 or 1976, but the idea was planted.

The Port itself, needing more revenue, raised its tariff. This brought quick reaction from stevedoring companies, ship agencies, and dock workers, all of which complained that it would drive off Port customers.

The dockage and wharfage fees were the heart of the matter. Dockage is a charge against a ship's size (e.g., four cents per gross registered ton per day); wharfage is a charge against the cargo (e.g., fifty cents per gross ton hauled across docks). The Port wanted to lower both and eliminate the provision that wharfage never exceed dockage charges. Opponents said that that would in effect increase charges sharply on vessels carrying small tonnage, thus encouraging them to dock elsewhere.

The Ships

The Yugoslav motor vessel *Alka* was the first foreign ship to dock in 1976. She tied up on April 7 to unload marble, wine, and machinery from the Mediterranean and Adriatic.

Incoming traffic was good. The Lykes Line was especially valued as one of only two U.S. ocean carriers working the Seaway. Their vessel, the *Ashley Lykes,* came in April 22 and picked up a large load of Gould components for the building of a $47-million diesel engine bearings plant at Dimitravgras on the Volga.

The Lykes Line's personality was visible even to strangers. It named its vessels for family women, and it valued experienced captains. Harold Mason, master of the valuable *Ashley Lykes,* was the face of a truly ancient mariner.

By June, tonnage was well ahead of 1975, and there was time to enjoy the invasion of the tall ships. First in was the majestic three-masted Norwegian windjammer *Christian Radich.* Thousands of Clevelanders lined the shore and the decks of scores of small motor yachts to stare in awe as the beautiful monster whispered up to Dock 34 and threw off lines. Four helicopters buzzed her rigging.

Chief Mate Jan Fjeld-Hansen looked at the huge crowd and shook his head. "She is special," he said softly, "but not *that special.*"

She was followed by the Canadians *Pathfinder* and *Playfair.*

Port business continued strong. Cargo handled was just short of a half-million tons by the end of November, up 25 percent over the same period last year. Revenues were up 57 percent. A large part of that was from storage and demurrage charges (penalty charge for freight overstays on railroad cars, on docks, or in warehouses). The business of the Port showed use by 198 ships. Container business remained minimal.

The 1976 record was good, but

Painchaud, with his flair for presentation, enhanced the gain by not mentioning the previous down season and by predicting that the Port would turn its first profit in 1977. The Port's equity rose in 1976 by $511,000.

Business continued strong. During the weekend before Thanksgiving, eight foreign vessels were berthed in the Port. And they were in a hurry. Despite the talk about year-round operation, John Kroon, manager of operating services for the Seaway, sent messages that waters at St. Lambert Lock, always the first to freeze, were down to thirty-five degrees. On November 23 there were still ninety-four ocean ships in the system, sixty-seven still above Port Weller in western Lake Ontario. The Seaway was scheduled to close December 18, and the Welland on December 30.

By November 24 ice was forming on the edges of the St. Lawrence.

Meanwhile Back at the Office ...

In the spring of 1976, the Port had become local coordinator for the Site 14 spoils disposal dike, and that summer the Corps of Engineers had requested that the Port be the coordinating agency for another needed disposal dike. The Board agreed, providing it inherited no great responsibility for maintenance.

Some heartburn developed over the much-delayed leasing of Warehouse A to the Cast Equipment Division of the Combustion Engineering Company. Strong protests rose, objections that this was not a water-related tenant and would not furnish work for longshoremen. Strikes and other measures were threatened. Chairman Bernstein explained the intense and protracted effort that had produced only this tenant. Rent was to rise annually from a beginning $117,355.

In considering purchase of the adjacent property, including the Parcel Post Building, the Board ran into sharp disagreement. Ultimately they decided *not* to mount a 1976 levy effort for purchase of the property.

In the fall of 1976, the Port applied for funds from the Economic Development Administration for construction of a marine containers terminal and a direct handling bulk cargo facility.

The 1976 season's last ship into Cleveland, the Brazilian *Joana*, struck and damaged the dock. There was great concern about all ocean ships getting out to the ocean before the freeze, but they all made it. The *Attica* was the last to clear the St. Lambert Lock.

The Port Authority had done a superb job of pushing for more space for more shipping and of coping with hard politics that threatened elimination of the Port Authority. That would seem to be the most severe test. Just as the Port planned its largest yet single move to lift Port business to a new level, it ran into challenges in 1977–78 that would make the previous experience as tame as church softball.

10

Great Expectations, 1977–1978

For a change, even before the ice softened, 1977 prospects looked superb for the Port's tonnage. Beyond that, the directors made their strongest reach thus far for two long-range income producers: a Cleveland free trade zone and a bulk cargo dock to gain the thousand-footer business, which would require expanding the property again.

In January, however, as the Authority prepared for its own levy campaign, various maritime interests began protesting proposed major increases in Seaway and Welland charges. All maritime levels, from longshoremen to agents and shippers and all the way up to top federal officials, ran up storm signals. Most claimed the raises would devastate the Great Lakes maritime economy.

The argument dominated 1977 until mid-December when U.S. and Canadian officials reached an agreement, albeit an unpopular one. The toll increases would remain high, as proposed, but would take place over three years, half the increase coming in 1978. The ultimate raise would nearly double the charges for a fully loaded ship.

The drive to establish a bulk cargo pier large enough to service the new supercarriers was supported widely, but not deeply enough. The supporters farthest from the water's edge assumed that the Port had no competition in this matter. The project needed enough land to accommodate the new jumbo carriers, vessels longer than three football fields; it also needed a viable plan for getting the bulk cargo up the Cuyahoga to the steel mills. And it needed the aggressive support of all the city leadership, because the port at Lorain already had such dock accommodations for the big vessels. Lorain was desperate for the business and would fight for it.

Operations

The shipping season got a late start in 1977. Mother Nature laughed at mankind's year-round navigation demonstration project. Six weeks early, Lake Erie froze shore to shore a foot deep, five in some places. Lake Michigan froze thirty-six miles out, and most of western Lake Superior froze. Oil tankers delivering necessary heating oil in Lake Michigan diverted ice breakers from other trades. And the Seaway leadership announced it would open later in 1978.

On April 13, about 150 Ohio dignitaries went down to Dock 26 to greet the first ship, the West German *Paul L. Russ,* commanded by Captain Werner Kumbartsky. He brought steel wire, brass tubing, auto parts, furniture, linoleum, and cheeses. The *Russ* made other deliveries on the Lakes and returned to Cleveland to pick up stainless steel sheets, automobiles, and logs for Europe.

The *Russ* opened a season of optimism. News came that Great Lakes & European Lines would make Cleveland a regular port of call.

The beautiful, deluxe French *Eglantine* brought in 11,200 tons of coiled steel from Holland. The elegant freighter with carpeted quarters had a pool for the crew. (They said they could not fill the pool from Lake Erie water because it was not clean enough.)

In June the Italian *Golfo di Palo* tied up. Again, the Port was embarrassed because Immigration would not permit crew ashore; the paperwork was not in order. The captain explained that Norfolk, New Orleans, and Tampa had granted waivers. However, Bert C. Rizzo, from Immigration, responded to the intervening Italian consul (who drove up from Columbus) that those waivers were irrelevant. "This is Cleveland, and we enforce the law." While the Port marketing effort reached for foreign business, the other hand of government pushed it away.

By July, Port executives knew they were going to have a good tonnage year. Painchaud reported to the Board, "Since the first ship, two hundred thirty-four thousand, eight hundred sixty-seven tons have been handled." That was nearly 100,000 tons better than the previous same period, a 71-percent improvement.

The Port's capability improved dramatically when Great Lakes International, a stevedoring company, installed an enormous mobile crane rated at 250 tons (100 tons more than the Buckeye Booster). The massive crane, the largest on the Lakes, walked the dock on 26-foot crawlers, and the arm had a 50-yard reach. Its two diesels developed 1,000 horsepower. Great Lakes International was formed by George Steinbrenner as an American Shipbuilding subsidiary. It operated six heavy duty cranes and thirty-six forklifts.

The Port continued the uphill search for container business. Container business disturbed the ILA nationally because it used fewer longshoremen. It also felt threatened by two other oncoming methods, LASH and RO-RO. LASH means "lighter aboard ship." Such a vessel carries stacks of loaded barges to be put over the side to enter a shallow harbor or river. RO-RO means "roll-on, roll-off." Loaded trucks roll aboard ship and roll off at destination, driving their cargoes directly to the consignees without stevedore help.

The tonnage was rolling across the docks better than in any previous year. By the end of August, the record had already been broken: 455,713 tons, a 52-percent gain over 1976. August alone showed a 62-percent gain.

This success highlighted some bad news. The *Tensha Maru No. 1* lay along Dock 24 offloading thousands of tons of coiled wire rod from Japan. That symbolized the 1977 Port success and 1977 American steel industry distress. "That penetration is on the way from 15 percent to 30 percent," claimed Edgar Speer, head of U.S. Steel, "and could cost ninety-six thousand American steel jobs."

Cleveland, Lorain, Youngstown, Warren, and Massillon are steel towns hurt by imports.

Ports Are People

On February 15, 1977, men on the Port security force were kidding Captain Joseph M. Ippoliti, head of the security force: "Just twelve days to go, Joe!"

Captain Ippoliti had once headed security for the Cleveland Public Library system, St. Lukes Hospital, and the Cleveland Pneumatic Company before being assigned by Able Security Company to the Port.

Today his colleagues were counting down: twelve days to his seventieth birthday, when he looked forward to retiring. But on the afternoon of February 15, he was struck down by a heart attack.

Near the end of the year, November 3, 1977, Christopher J. Howley, Port operations manager, was driving into the Port from his home in Sheffield, Ohio. Suddenly he pulled his car off onto the berm. A paramedic in a car behind him noticed the maneuver and stopped. He ran to Howley's car and found him collapsed over the wheel. It was too late for first aid.

Chris Howley began a maritime career on the decks of the Columbia Fleet. In World War II he was a naval lieutenant commander, serving in both the Atlantic and Pacific. After the war, he became vice president of Oglebay Norton. He was a founder and president of Great Lakes Terminals Association and represented Cleveland on the Great Lakes Task Force.

On the evening of June 27, the chauffeured Lincoln of Port director John J. (Skip) Felice, Jr., drew up to 101 Erieside, Port headquarters. As he and his bodyguard stepped out of the limousine, *Cleveland Press* photographer Tony Tomasic, waiting there on assignment, photographed Felice, who was also an officer in three teamster locals.

Tomasic was assigned to get the photographs because Felice was under investigation for possible embezzlement of union funds. Felice rushed Tomasic, grabbed the camera, wrapped the strap around Tomasic's neck, and tried to confiscate the film. Unable to get the film out of the camera, Felice yanked on the strap around Tomasic's neck until the latter delivered the film. "I was not about to fight those two guys."

Plans, Plans, Plans

One July evening Alan Kuper and a handful of Sierra Club members, looking to make the shoreline more useful to the public, took a walk.

From the pavilion at Edgewater Park we walked through a wide-open patch of green grass, passed a sandy beach with children playing and a pier crowded with evening fishermen. All too soon then we came upon an expanse of land littered with broken bottles and stones. We navigated through beer cans, broken bricks and glass.

From there our path led east passing Western Sewage Disposal toward Whiskey Island and a debris-filled jungle . . . shoes, furniture, tires. We have one of the most valuable resources in the country, and it's up to us to put it to the very best use. Not a dump.

The Sierra Club was only one of a dozen civic organizations planning a better lakefront.

Meanwhile, at the Port and at City Hall plans were ongoing for a foreign trade zone.

The big high-potential plan, however, was for an ore dock. And real progress was made. The Port directors gave a go-ahead in December 1977 to plans for a $20 million ore dock, authorizing the Port to purchase the Post Office Annex on Dock 20. James Carney, chairing the finance committee, said that the Port had a firm deal to buy the annex for about $4.5 million and to buy the dock from Penn Central for $1.5 million. The proposed dock would accommodate the new supercarriers.

The directors also signed a letter of intent with Republic Steel Corporation in which Republic agreed to underwrite financing except for the first $3.5 million and any possible federal funding from a potential EDA grant. Republic would pay two cents per ton of ore unloaded at the dock. The company generally used about six million tons of bulk material yearly, most of it iron ore.

In October the levy campaign group headed by William King of the Cleveland Electric Illuminating Company (CEI) and J. Madigan of Madigan Associates earned cooperation of all media to hammer on the jobs theme. The lead of Stephen Blossom's October 17 feature in the *Plain Dealer:* "One of Cleveland's best kept secrets is the fact that its port is responsible indirectly for over 100,000 jobs and a cash flow of $450 million."

The rationale may have been shaky in claiming 40,000 local *manufacturing* jobs made possible by the Port. Those companies would have been in business with or without the Port, but the Port was a significant help.

The levy passed 243,586 to 180,561.

That, plus the record tonnage, made 1977 a good year.

The Canadian Seaway Authority warned all ocean ships that they could get trapped in the Lakes by a December 15 closing. On December 3, the Port was alive with ships and trucks as ocean vessels hurried to escape. Twelve days was not a safe margin, since pilotage restrictions at the Welland in heavy traffic make a bottleneck, and wind and fog can slow or halt traffic.

In the rush to escape, many downbound vessels bypassed Cleveland, leaving much outbound cargo stranded here, including a large fleet of Euclid off-highway trucks, walnut logs, cranes, cars, and machinery. They would find other modes.

On December 15 the Brazilian *Caicara* was hurrying to load at Cleveland, still hoping to get out of the Lakes for Rio.

The Canadian Seaway Authority had announced that vessels arriving at Checkpoint Whaleback (near Brockville, downstream on Lake Ontario) before midnight December 16 would be guaranteed passage out of the Seaway, but those arriving later would have no guarantee.

The *Caicara* cast off before noon on December 15, the last ocean vessel out of Cleveland in 1977. By a combination of lucky breaks, she made it to saltwater.

The 1978 outlook appeared good for repeating last year's prosperity, which saw record tonnage, a successful levy, and a honeymoon with new mayor Dennis Kucinich. Good news was that the U.S. flag carrier *Lykes Brothers* had decided to increase its sailings into the Great Lakes. Chairman Bernstein prophesied three hundred ships for 1978. The Port's tax anticipation notes received a top rating from Moody's financial rating service. If such good luck continued, the plans for the ore dock and Post Office Annex purchase would advance.

In an optimistic mood that winter, the Port directors and managers discussed the possibility of replacing the Buckeye Booster with a more mobile crane.

The Board was pleased with the plans presented by the Orba Company for the new ore dock, plans that carefully provided for pollution controls. The media carried existing artist drawings of the planned ore dock. Mayor Dennis Kucinich, boyish in appearance and stature, applauded the plan. The future ore dock was considered such a sure thing that the Sierra Club asked for a public observation platform to overlook the new facility.

On April 9, Captain Zunic Rouko sailed the Yugoslavian *Makarska* into Cleveland with 420 tons of aluminum ingots.

Tonnage was up. April was 46 percent ahead of April 1977, a record-breaking year. So things seemed to be going very well.

Who could predict that into that promising picture would plunge a steel pricing trigger regulation, some surprise personnel changes, and a political battle hostile to the Port?

In spring, vague uneasiness crept in. The new mayor, who had written a cordial letter of support to the Port Authority Board, now announced opposition to recreational development of the lakefront, including the museum proposed by the Great Lakes Historical Society and the proposed but delayed Gateway complex. The lakefront was to be for industry use.

Although young, Mayor Kucinich, having served on City Council and run for Congress, was already politically seasoned. He brought into office with him a very young and eager corps of campaigners plus one veteran gatekeeper, Bob Weisman, formerly with the United Auto Workers (UAW). Most of these individuals shared the attitude on which their chief campaigned, a battle cry of the little man against big business and entrenched institutions. However, some of his team, riding a wave of victory, did not have Kucinich's experience and implemented new policy with insensitive arrogance that boomeranged. In backing up the actions of his young tigers, the mayor came head to head with many bureaus, departments, commissioners, business leaders, and especially the physically and politically towering

Council president, George Forbes.

Caught in this crossfire was the Port Authority.

The mayor's brash young administration talked about a higher rent to be paid by the Port to the city. There was unofficial, but threatening, talk about the city taking back the Port altogether.

That spring, Robert Bennett and A. Sapienza came to the end of their Board terms. By the rules, however, directors served until their replacements arrived. Mayor Kucinich appointed Warren Davis of the United Auto Workers and Charles Miller, a previous holder of several political appointments. These appointments needed Council approval, which was not forthcoming; hence, Bennett and Sapienza continued.

At midyear a lease with the city for Dock 24 had passed through City Council but was awaiting the Kucinich signature. Kucinich was not a friend of the Board's Bennett or Carney. He held up approval of several important Port matters. By late July, the mayor was subject of a recall action, and the business of the city stalled.

The mayor's fiscal policies brought the city to the brink of bankruptcy. Seeking potential extra income, his staff demanded an increase in the Port rent, backed by a threat of taking back the docks and disbanding the Port Authority. Chairman Bernstein retaliated toe to toe in the media and by lobbying City Council.

Trigger Price

In February 1978, the Carter administration announced a steel trigger-pricing mechanism: if a ton of imported steel fell below a specific price, it would trigger a Department of Treasury investigation into whether the import steel was being illegally dumped (sold here for less than in its own country). Painchaud told the *Plain Dealer,* "The trigger prices, as now established, effectively embargo Great Lakes ports out of the import steel business. We're going to get hurt, there's no question about it."

Musical Chairs

The Authority had some personnel shocks in 1978. Ports are never the most pious precinct in town. Nevertheless, many Clevelanders were stunned at the end of April to learn that Port Board member Skip Felice was indicted for conspiracy to murder a union rival and for misusing his union's funds extensively. He was charged with plotting to murder Teamsters business agent Manuel J. Colta, Jr., who was shot in the face in Lyndhurst on December 29, 1977. Felice was considered the only serious threat to the Presser family's reign over Ohio Teamsters.

In June, Executive Director Painchaud suddenly sent a letter of resignation by messenger to Chairman Bernstein and made himself immediately unavailable for comment. Jack Hively again became acting executive director.

On September 8, in the midst of complaints that Councilman Russo had persuaded five of the Port directors to appoint his father executive director, the Port engineer, John Wolf, resigned. Wolf had been a good influence on the Board.

Councilman Russo claimed that he never approached the directors on behalf of his father. Press editorials, however, claimed that this kind of political football with the Port management was supposed to be eliminated by creation of the Authority and that Tony Russo's one-year experience with the old port in no way qualified him to be director of this largest Ohio port operation.

In November, the Board's selection committee recommended that acting director Jack Hively become executive director and that Tony Russo become deputy director.

Foreign Trade Zone

The establishment of a foreign trade zone remained important to the Board and the city as a way to increase Port tonnage. A foreign trade zone license ropes off an area within which a domestic manufacturer can import parts duty free if the intent is to assemble them into a product that will then be immediately exported. The Authority had been negotiating for a half year through the federal approval process involved in acquiring this license.

In October 1978, the Department of Commerce approved the application. The Port Board appointed a foreign trade zone committee: Jay Ehle as chairman and Joseph Bartunek, James Carney, and Loran Hammett.

The Ore Dock

The dream of the ore dock was promising. Republic Steel, the prospective chief customer, had kept its part of the bargain, advancing $3.5 million, and agreeing to other terms. The Port Authority agreed to pay the city $100,000 a year rent for Dock 20 on the Cuyahoga. City Council favored the whole arrangement.

To show Cleveland citizens the spectacular size of the new jumbo bulk carriers, the *Barker* made a slow cruise of the waterfront. Even sophisticated maritimers found her awesome.

Suddenly Cleveland law director Jack Schulmann, the negotiator for the city, said the dock space was worth $150,000 per year. Mayor Kucinich, whose charm for some was his anti–big business stance, charged that the Port's arrangement with Republic was subsidizing the steel company. Kucinich delayed granting the lease for the ore dock.

On June 20, steelworker union members left a Kucinich speech to protest dock delay. By July 3, Kucinich had shut down the dock plans.

On July 10 the Council president cut off Kucinich in debate. The mayor stormed out of the chamber. Standard & Poor suspended the city's bond rating.

Council approved the dock lease over the mayor's protests.

On July 10 another confrontation occurred in Council over the dock issue.

Kucinich said, "I determine the issue."

Forbes responded, "Not in this chamber."

Kucinich and his cabinet walked out.

On July 19 the mayor vetoed the lease for the Republic ore dock.

On August 17, Republic Steel raised its offer. And on September 8, the *Cleveland Press* carried the headline: "WE'VE GOT A DEAL TO BUILD ORE DOCK! Mayor and Forbes Meet for an Hour. Mayor Will Sign."

However, Republic Steel management did not believe it could trust on-off Kucinich.

Therefore, the December 24 *Plain Dealer* headline closed the story: "A Tangled Tale: How City Lost the Ore Dock to Lorain."

11

A Three-Year Siege, 1979–1981

Our Port Authority should be disbanded.
—County Commissioner Sweeney

County and City vs. Port

At her crowded desk in the Port office, Mary Sherman, now assistant to the executive director, covered the back of a *Plain Dealer* clipping with rubber cement and carefully pasted it onto the last page (which is the front page) of a thick scrapbook labeled "1978." She shelved the scrapbook with a row of others.

Mary Sherman knew more about this Port than anyone. She still does. She was the only staff member who worked for the Port when it was city owned. In fourteen-point type this last 1978 clipping she had just filed asked how Cleveland could have lost this prize to Lorain.

If anyone had asked Sherman, she could have answered. But the headline causes one to wonder why successful men serve on public boards.

Chairman Bernstein, to succeed in businesses, including the quality restaurant business, was necessarily a gregarious, optimistic executive. However, it required a stiff upper lip for him, entering 1979 after that ore dock headline, to open the first Board meeting with a review of 1978.

Yet there were some accomplishments: the foreign trade zone license; dock resurfacing; a new guardhouse; the retirement of the $2.5 million tax anticipation notes.

And although 1978 volume was off 28 percent, that was against a previous record year. Additionally, the new trigger pricing hurt steel imports.

Loren Hammett, maritime knowledgeable and conservative in forecasting, reported that there was still some hope for a new iron ore dock for the big self-unloaders via modernization of Conrail's dock on Whiskey Island, managed by the Hanna Company.

Why modernization? The blizzard of 1978 destroyed the big ore bridge. Therefore, ore had been handled by earthmoving equipment, double and triple handling. This inefficient system would be replaced by a dock where self-unloaders could deposit ore directly into a big hopper; a wide belt would then convey pellets to storage. Another would load ore into railcars. Although costly to build and install (approximately $20 million), operating costs would drop.

However, since all but $245,000 of the $13-million budget of the Army Corps of Engineers was already promised for annual dredging and rehabilitating the western breakwall, another source of funding would be needed.

While enjoying that upbeat potential, the Board also knew there were some hungry alligators under the table. James Carney reminded members that the Authority would now need to repay Republic's $3.5-million advance to buy Dock 20.

And prospects for an early sailing season? For the first time since the Seaway, Mother Nature froze over each of the Lakes.

And the possibility of the vaunted year-round navigation? New York and the Atlantic states would successfully block spending $1.5 billion to keep shipping lanes open year-round just to benefit a few Midwest companies.

Facing Great Lakes Realities

While the Board, like all port boards, was comprised of highly political men whose prime career interest was not waterborne shipping, it also contained four who knew the Lakes. Ehle and Hammett were professionally involved in lake transport; Carney, a quick study in any business, was on the Board from the first, and Bernstein was now experienced in the facts of maritime business.

Picture the challenge, then, to a knowledgeable Great Lakes port executive director or board as the 1980s approached. Out of 1,400 U.S. flag sailings per year, only a dozen originated or terminated at Great Lakes ports, a region accounting for a third of the U.S. gross national product and a quarter of U.S. exports. Yet no vessels were being built to fit the Seaway, and, while the government required that 40 percent of exports go in U.S. ships, less than 1 percent of U.S. flags served the Great Lakes.

Additionally, the Seaway shut out foreign trade by closing around December 15, and it pushed business to coastal ports by raising Seaway charges 113 percent; a heavily loaded vessel might pay $35,000. Meanwhile, subsidized railroad rates pulled Midwest shipments to coastal ports.

The port director also knows he cannot become a large player in the dominating container shipping because big container vessels cannot squeeze into the Seaway upstream of Montreal. The sixteen locks that drop ships 602 feet from Lake Superior to Montreal restrict ship size (except for the Poe Lock).

And while the port director cannot get U.S. vessels to call, he is also losing foreign vessel lines. In an attempt to remedy this, the Cleveland Board supported a petition to the U.S. Department of Transportation for a subsidy for the Great Atlantic Steamship Company to establish regular Great Lakes service.

Meanwhile, political candidates, unfamiliar with marine realities, harked back to the original Seaway boosterism, and on campaign stumps they challenged, "What's wrong with our Port management?"

In February, the county commissioners appointed to the Port Board Martin J. Hughes to replace Anthony O. Calabrese, Jr. Hughes, the international vice president of the Communications Workers Union and a very effective union lobbyist in Washington, was considered a rising star in labor.

A Second Chance

Following the loss of the ore dock to Lorain, when Mayor Kucinich's attitude destroyed Republic Steel's confidence in the Cleveland Port, the Authority responded eagerly to news that Conrail was considering operating on its Whiskey Island property a large ore dock. The thousand-foot supercarriers could self-unload ore to be transshipped by rail to downstate steel mills. Conrail senior vice president James A. Hagen said, "While there is no firm timetable, we want to proceed as quickly as possible."

In March a *Cleveland Press* headline read: "Secret Pact Makes Dock Money-Maker for City!" It referred to a meeting of Bernstein, Calfee, and Carney with J & L Steel and that company's hauler. They proposed to use Dock 20 for bulk cargo to be handled by the Cleveland Stevedore Company. Expectations were for 18,000 tons per week at 40 cents per ton for the Authority. They kept the meeting small, fearing a leak that could quash the project, as had happened before.

"A Damn Shame!"

That was County Commissioner Timothy Hagan's reaction to Ohio

House Bill 628. This bill started a tremendous disruption that dominated the year for the Port and turned its two parents hostile.

House Bill 628 would expand the power of port authorities. It would empower them to purchase public property by eminent domain. They could contract with public or private groups to build recreational facilities on port properties with certain tax benefits. They could issue bonds without a vote of the people. They could override a port's allowed indebtedness.

In short, it made port authorities so powerful that it raised the hackles of all the Port's enemies and some of its friends. The city and the county feared creation of a political monster.

County Commissioner Edward Feighan pressured the Port to drop its support for the bill. He vowed to kill the bill, "when and if it reaches the Senate." Hagan urged the county legislative delegation to oppose.

Opposition to the bill brought Mayor Kucinich and Commissioners Feighan and Hagan into unlikely alliance against the Port Authority. Feighan declared, "It's another clear example of why appointed boards are not in the best interests of the public." He pledged to curb power of all unelected boards.

In another weird political twist, the argument pitted Feighan and Hagan against Jim Carney.

Opponents dubbed H.B. 628 "The Port Landgrab Bill."

In June, the bill (minus the power of eminent domain) quietly passed the House 69 to 27; the Cuyahoga County delegation split 8 to 6.

In the June 22 *Plain Dealer,* Board member Martin J. Hughes said, "Port Authority plans call for a $7 million dollar improvement to Dock 20 on the Cuyahoga; $2.5 million for the world trade zone area; $2.5 million for Docks 32 and 34 near the East 9th Street Pier."

Many civic bodies, including the Citizens League, jumped in to kill the bill in the Senate.

"Dissolve the Port Authority"

Kucinich's response to the passage in the House was to urge city and county officials to dissolve the Port Authority and return control of the Port to the "elected officials at City Hall."

The *Plain Dealer* pinned House passage on the shoulders of Port Deputy Director Anthony J. Russo, who had five terms of experience in the Ohio House.

Kucinich, Feighan, and Hagan moved their fight to the Ohio Senate, where the bill would be considered in the fall. In July County Commission president Robert E. Sweeney threatened to disband the Port Authority if it continued to back the legislation. He staged a public hearing in August to support his threat.

Over the summer, Port directors met with all the protesting groups. Bartunek reported back on his meeting with the Citizens League: "The questions regarding tax abatement on land improvements and recreation facilities and issuance of bonds without voter approval must be solved first, and if questions are justified the bill should be amended." Bartunek made conciliatory comments to the *Press* regarding the city and county officials.

Following in-depth analysis of H.B. 628 by the Port's long-range planning and the development committees and its legal counsel, Bartunek's recommendation to the Board was not to support the bill in its present form (Hughes was the only nay vote). Despite politics, fuel shortage, dwindling U.S. flag vessels, and a short season, tonnage for the first six months was 79 percent ahead and, by August 31, 120 percent ahead.

On the Waterfront

The elegant 37,000-ton French *Eglantine* opened the Port in April. Captain Francois Sornec said they came through the great storm on Lake Ontario without serious problems. As one of the very few French ships calling in Cleveland, the *Eglantine* was very popular.

Some interesting cargoes came. An elegant English road carriage that was over one hundred years old and seated sixteen people shipped out for England. Two fairly new naval frigates visited, the USS *Fairfax* and the *Oliver Hazard Perry*, inviting the public aboard. Terex shipped millions of dollars worth of off-highway mining trucks to Argentina.

One ship bypassed the docks and hauled up the Cuyahoga to the Cleveland Builders Supply dock because it could unload tanks too large to be ground transported on trucks through the city. People, including media, who did not know that logistics problem, charged that since Cleveland Builders was the company of Jay Ehle, Port Board member, the CBS dock should not have been used for this shipment.

During a paper mill strike, newspapers were forced to import rolls of newsprint. The *Cleveland Press,* for example, used about 600 tons a week. Ten thousand rolls entered Cleveland's Port in 1979.

Physical Plant and Man-Made Land

The Corps of Engineers, in a major project, was increasing the lakefront just east of Burke Lakefront Airport. They built a rubble-mound breakwater for a dike enclosure and a 20,000-foot extension of a storm run-off culvert. The Corps would fill the impoundment with dredge spoil to create eighty-eight acres of new park land.

For the Cleveland breakwater rehabilitation, subcontractor Alpha Precast was manufacturing 29,500 anchorlike devices (dolos) to be positioned in a double layer across the 4,400-foot-long underwater face of the breakwall, interlocking against wave action. This was the first Great Lakes use of these devices.

Remodeling the Parcel Post Building to convert it to a Free Trade Zone was challenging, because the 118,000-square-foot space was designed around railroad mail car use. After reviewing the plans and bids, the Board approved the action ($85,000 budget), Hughes dissenting.

At year-end, the Authority authorized issue of $2,200,000 refunding revenue bonds to refund all outstanding Port bonds.

Two veteran Board members died in 1979, John G. Pegg, one of the earliest directors, and Harry F. Burmester, the first chairman.

The Big Turnover

Struggling against a stiff breeze on her deck-load of containers, the *Lindo* tied up to Dock 24E, opening the 1980 season on April 4. A real international, she hailed from Dublin under a German captain, Herbert Nitschke. Manned by Asians, she was chartered by a British company. The Port went to work for the 1980 season.

Backstage of the actual shipping work, the Authority management dispatched some of the time-consuming administrative work people don't see from the water. For example, it authorized bids taken for the Free Trade Zone tenants. After years of negotiation, the Authority paid taxes on Dock 20. It also prepared an affirmative action program and applied for an EDA grant.

Such behind-the-docks work goes on year-round. Periodically, and with good reason in this litigious marine business, directors became concerned about personal liability. The Port's outside counsel advised, however, that it was not legal to have the Authority buy liability insurance for directors and officers.

The Authority studied the Corps of Engineers winter navigation investigation. The document claimed that a twelve-month season was feasible but would require a paint lockerfull of money to improve certain channels and increase ice-breaking capability.

The battle over H.B. 628 bridged across into 1980. As the bill moved into Ohio Senate hearings, County Commissioner Sweeney stepped up his campaign to kill it, declaring that if it becomes law, "our Port Authority should be disbanded." His timing was damaging because the Authority's defenses were about to be weakened dramatically.

The dynamic James Carney, veteran of the very first Board and a real advocate and action leader, left the Board upon his term expiration. Beyond the official perfunctory farewell, Carney received the more meaningful informed thanks of maritime insiders who really knew Carney's impact. The Board lost a tiger.

The city and the county also had a better chance to control the Port because of the approaching ends-of-term of several directors. A jarring turnover of appointees left Bernstein and Ehle as the two veteran directors. Hughes was strong but fairly new, and suddenly six new appointees came aboard. While these were very worldly men, experienced in business and politics, they were not maritime men. Sheldon Schecter and Joseph Berger were attorneys; Otis Moss, a minister; Arnold Pinkney, an insurance entrepreneur and politician; Campbell Elliott, a businessman and former head of the Cleveland Growth Association; Stefan Deubel, the publisher of a German-language periodical. They owed their appointments to two government bodies that were eager to disband the Authority.

On this radically new Board, Bernstein, Ehle, and Hughes remained chairman, secretary-treasurer, and vice chairman, respectively. Ehle also chaired the operations and personnel committee.

"The Port Is Practically out of Business"

A recession fogged the waterfront. Autos were down. Steel down. April tonnage was down 11 percent. Only a third of longshoremen were working. The Port was selling and leasing out some equipment.

The Authority reached for new business. The Regional Transit Authority (RTA) had ordered forty-eight railcars, manufactured in Italy by Breda Construzioni. Aggressively, the Port tried every way to have those cars routed through this Port, but RTA's contract gave the manufacturer full control of shipping. Breda claimed shipping through Baltimore much more economical; however, they would consider Cleveland if a case could be made. RTA gave the Port good opportunity to come up with competitive cost estimates. New director Arnold Pinkney made an impassioned effort, claiming RTA had a moral obligation to demand that the cars be shipped through Cleveland's Port. But he was not yet familiar with the logistic realities of ship size, Welland size, federal requirements, and freezing of the waters.

Every port exists in a constant intergovernmental tension. In spring, the State of Ohio sued Cleveland for taking over the abandoned Coast Guard station and leasing it to the Port. All underwater land belonged to the state, they said. The federal government had quitclaimed it to Cleveland. The city leased it to the Port and installed in it the city's Water Pollution Board.

May tonnage was down 12 percent. "The Great Lakes are really hurting," said Francis Coakley, vice president of Cleveland Stevedore Company. "Even the ships which do call have less tonnage."

While imported steel shipments fell, the drop was offset some for the Port by a rise in iron ore handling for Jones & Laughlin.

In July, tonnage for the year was down 54 percent. Compounding the Port's sales problem was another increase in Seaway tolls. Chicago was also down 70 percent, Detroit 43 percent, Duluth 19 percent. A slack auto industry hurt all Lakes ports.

The slow business was food for politician critics. The best port manager in the world cannot widen the Welland, change restrictive federal regulations, create cargoes that have not been manufactured. Nor could he reverse the embargo that cut out an average of forty-five Russian ships that had been calling at Cleveland.

County Commissioner Sweeney used the low tonnage to resume his assault, this time charging poor management.

The three veteran directors had already learned that a port becomes a whipping boy for hard times, and they could stand the heat in the galley. However, some newer directors could not. They partially joined the critics. They proposed grand plans for attacking stone walls, then bounced off them with some bruises that sent them retreating into side-issue administrative details with no strong directions.

Sweeney declared to the media, "The Port is practically out of business." He called for a complete management review. With TV crew in tow, he made an unannounced visit to the Port, pulling rank on the gate guard.

John Baker of ILA Local 1317 also criticized, "The director and his sales force are not doing the job. And the Board doesn't go out and seek someone who can."

Sweeney planned to meet with the new mayor, George Voinovich, to create an aggressive program to revitalize the Port. "We can't sit by and see this great potential go to waste. We need to take a whole new look. It is unbelievable when you look at the figures."

He cited six local companies "who should be using the Port." The named companies responded angrily, showing valid reasons why they did not use the Port.

The year 1979 closed with the Port under assault from many powerful quarters. Mayor Voinovich, having visited Baltimore's booming port, was reportedly tilting toward Sweeney's threat to disband the Authority and take the Port back into city or county government.

Despite the attack, the Port Authority, paying its bills, including $400,000 a year rent to the city, was in sound financial condition.

You Can't Please All of the People All of the Time

In 1980 the officers and directors would be even more severely tested by a year of negotiations and complicated agreements, falling economy, hostile press, and a search for a new director.

First order of business concerned a lease agreement for Dock 20 with Lake Erie Asphalt Products, Inc. This would take several months to resolve. In Lake Erie Asphalt's attempt to remain competitive (particularly with Pinney Dock & Transport Company in Ashtabula, which was not charging carriers for dock storage and rehandling), the company requested reduction in storage charges on Dock 20. Accommodating this request would require an addendum to the original lease.

Board members debated whether a discussion of this could even be held publicly, as some of the facts were submitted in confidence. Martin Hughes succinctly challenged, "Does the Cleveland–Cuyahoga County Port Authority have the authority, without the revenue bond holder approval, to make a change in the lease agreement which would result in a reduction?"

Arnold Pinkney felt that it was not any business of the revenue bond holders and that legal counsel for the Port should establish guidelines on the Sunshine Law as related to this negotiation.

And there *was* a confidential aspect because of discrepancies between tonnage figures from Lake Erie Asphalt's customer, Jones & Laughlin Steel, and those reported by Lake Erie Asphalt to the Port. The Board asked an independent auditor to review computer sheets and submit results to counsel.

Searching

In January the Board appointed the engineering firm of Tippetts-Abbett-McCarthy-Stratton (TAMS) as consultant for the Port development study. The first advisory committee meeting was held the following week to solicit recommendations from the public for Port revitalization.

As part of this, the Authority considered financing construction of a floating dry dock upriver in the Cuyahoga where it would be unaffected by ice and remain operational year-round. G&W Industries, which volunteered to pay for the feasibility study, had previously agreed to lease the completed dry dock. At the end of the lease, the dock would revert to the Port. Ehle moved, and won approval, to proceed with building a dry dock (one 150-foot section at $2 million and two 50-foot sections for $1.5 million).

Also ongoing was the Cleveland Harbor model study by the Corps of Engineers. The main consideration was construction of an all-weather east entrance to the Cleveland Harbor to improve conditions for docking vessels. Estimates ran high—$60–70 million.

Winds of Change

The real action took place following that January 12 meeting when the Board convened in executive session at a local restaurant. Since the three-hour session was to have focused on the 11-percent reduction in shipping and the 50-percent drop in international cargo, the *Cleveland Press* had expected an announcement that the Port's executive director had been fired. In thinly veiled disappointment they stated, "Port director Jack Hively was reportedly raked over the coals."

Bernstein spoke to the *Cleveland Press:* "We told [Hively] we wanted the port beefed up and more sales." He admitted the grim economy and prospects.

Robert W. Greshem, Jr., president of A. W. Fenton Company ("We're a travel agent for freight"), located in Brookpark, told *Crain's Cleveland Business,* "It's just quite frankly, too costly to operate ships on the Great Lakes." He cited long traveling time through the Seaway and the added cost of tolls and another major point: "If people were appointed to the Port Authority board because of their concern for Cleveland and its port, and not because of the buddy system or politics, we could have a good board."

However, Greshem predicted a big year for exporting due to poor domestic business conditions.

But it would be a hard sell for Hively, because he would have to counter a negative news media. Channel 5's Eyewitness News ran ads in the newspapers promoting "Port of Cleveland: Situation Critical," using a graphic illustration and the headline "WHO PULLED THE PLUG ON THE PORT?"

The same week, the *Plain Dealer* quoted Jerry Gobrecht, Chessie System executive: "The cost of shipping a ton of coal from eastern Kentucky to Europe via the Great Lakes and the seaway would be about $26 a ton [as opposed to] shipping from Kentucky through the ocean port of Newport News, Virginia . . . [at] about $14.60 a ton . . . [or] sending coal on the Ohio River and down the Mississippi River to News Orleans for overseas shipment ... [at] about $20 a ton."

At the February meeting, Jack Hively presented a rough draft of an operating agreement with the Park Corporation to manage Foreign Free Trade Zone No. 40. The document was reviewed, discussed, revised, and given for final review to I. Joseph Berger and Sheldon D. Schecter, attorneys on the Board.

However, the operating agreement was far from final. Mayor Voinovich discussed the development of Dock 20 and the Foreign Free Trade Zone with Vice President George Bush; Thomas Duffy, Cleveland's lobbyist in Washington, investigated Seaway tolls; and Acting Director Russo tried to set up a trade agreement with Taiwan.

A few Board members, those who would not accept any small changes out of their immediate control, caused this agreement to be placed under the microscope repeatedly. On March 16, after innumerable revisions and legal reviews, the chairman called for a roll-call vote. Over the verbal protests of Hughes and Berger, the resolution passed, and the chairman was authorized to negotiate an operating agreement with Park Corporation to operate FFTZ No. 40.

Lance Johnson of the Park Corporation had suggested that negotiations choked because of the necessity of dealing with nine Board members. He asked Bernstein if just one Board member could negotiate with

him. Jay Ehle was appointed.

At Last

After working with attorneys, Lance Johnson and foreign free trade zone legal experts, Jay Ehle presented to the Board the revised operating agreement for Foreign Free Trade Zone No. 40. After four frustrating months, this agreement was approved, though over the continued objections of Hughes and Berger.

In September, at the request of the Park Corporation, the original agreement was reworked to incorporate a subzone at the Cleveland Tank Plant. Despite the usual one dissenter, this agreement sailed through.

Position Open

Jack Hively had been with General Motors and Addressograph-Multigraph before joining the Port Authority in 1968. He had been the Port's acting director three times from 1974 until his appointment as executive director on December 8, 1978.

On February 25, 1981 (less than two months after the infamous after-hours meeting), he submitted his resignation. The Board appointed Arnold Pinkney to chair the search committee.

Publicly, Anthony Russo, acting executive director, said the resignation "developed as a mutual understanding." But the Board had exerted pressure.

By July 28 the search had reduced a field of forty-eight to fourteen candidates. In September, six were personally interviewed; in October, the top three were presented to the Board.

The Board unanimously chose C. Thomas Burke as the new executive director to start work on December 1.

Burke had national experience. He had met Hubert Humphrey and Walter Mondale when he was executive director of the Seaway Port Authority of Duluth and they were U.S. senators, and, with Humphrey's help, Burke became the first U.S. port director (Port of Duluth, 1969–77) to meet with Russian officials in the Soviet Union following the U.S.-Soviet Trade Agreement of 1972.

Burke accompanied Humphrey to the World Trade Conference in Rome as transportation consultant to the U.S. delegation. President Carter appointed Burke special assistant to the secretary of agriculture in 1977, and in 1979 Burke joined the State Department's Agency for International Development.

Burke had majored in transportation at Northeastern University in Boston and held a law degree from Blackstone School of Law in Chicago. His entire career had been transportation.

In Cleveland he planned to redefine the Port's marketing goals and

insisted that Cleveland consider Baltimore its biggest competitor rather than the other Great Lakes ports.

The Other Lease—Lake Erie Asphalt Products and Dock 20

The attention of the Board turned to a request by Ohio Bulk Transfer (OBT) to lease Dock 20, with OBT's promise of a better return than the Port was presently receiving from Lake Erie Asphalt Products, Inc. (LEAP).

This presented the Board with a combination legal/moral problem.

Calfee was asked to examine the validity of the Port's lease with LEAP; he advised that "a legal and viable lease agreement" did exist. John R. Climaco of Climaco, Seminatore, Lefkowitz & Kaplan, representing OBT, insisted that dating back to November 1980, his client had expressed interest in Dock 20; all correspondence had been ignored.

Climaco argued that someone other than Baker & Hostetler, Calfee's firm, should look at the lease—"with all due respect . . . they could be wrong."

At issue was Calfee's determination that the lease should be renegotiated *only* after the fourth year. Moreover, the yearly renegotiation in the lease referred *only* to the red shed, which rented out at $680 a month.

Climaco found this mysterious. Since the Port received $250,000 each year from the Dock 20 lease, why would they be spending any effort renegotiating a space that brings in only $7,800?

Calfee conceded that the renegotiation language was ambiguous but that its "intent is obvious ... the rate is to be $.40 per ton for the first four years." In addition, LEAP had not paid December's $200,000 fee within the calendar year, and some directors felt this constituted default. LEAP disagreed, claiming the standard thirty- to forty-five-day payment schedule on a bill would take payment for December into the next calendar year.

Hughes charged, "It looks like the ... Port Authority is avoiding accepting more revenue for the Port."

The Port was in a pickle. Abandoning LEAP for additional moneys offered by OBT might prompt Lake Erie Asphalt to sue. Sticking with the lease might prompt a taxpayer suit claiming the Port had shut out competition. Hughes wanted each contender to indemnify the Port if the vote favored their bid. Both refused.

Moss wanted to know if Board members might be held *personally* responsible.

The dilemma filled twenty-three pages of Board minutes. Finally Jay Ehle moved that the Board accept the opinion of the Port's legal counsel on the lease agreement with Lake Erie Asphalt Products, Inc.: "a legal agreement ... intent should be honored."

Over the objections of Hughes and Berger, with Moss withholding, the Board approved.

In April, Campbell Elliott became chairman of the Port's finance committee, replacing Martin Hughes. Hughes, who claimed he heard about his replacement as head of finance from a reporter, strongly defended his nonpayment of the Port's legal bills, saying Baker & Hostetler had been consistently overcharging the Port. Elliott, however, recommended paying all the Port's past-due legal bills for 1980 *immediately.* The Board concurred, minus Hughes and Berger.

The Ships

The first ship of 1981 was the Dutch MV *Katendrecht* on April 12.

The month of May saw several firsts for the Port of Cleveland: shipments of ferromanganese, tallow, and bauxite. After the Port received approval from the U.S. Department of Agriculture to handle shipments of wheat products, Cereal Foods Processors, Inc., began exporting shipments of flour milled at its facility in the Cleveland flats. Over 200,000 bags were handled through the Port in 1981.

By September, Port tonnage was 177 percent ahead, and there was optimism for increased Great Lakes trade with Canada. A small Canadian vessel would call at the Port every two

The Flats along the Cuyahoga, as seen from Scranton Heights. (Cleveland Press Collection/CSU Archives)

Whaleback barges late in the 1900 season at Duluth ore dock. These vessels, designed and built by Captain Alexander McDougall, were scorned (nicknamed "pig boats") until they proved to be excellent navigationally and commercially. Thirty-nine were built. One, the *Meteor*, worked until the 1960s hauling oil on Lake Michigan right through

Vessels daring to sail into November or early December risked taking on ice, sometimes over 150 tons. This ship is pictured late in the season at the Soo Locks, ca. 1920.

The new C&B and D&C terminals at East 9th Street, Cleveland 1915. Grand passenger vessels worked the Great Lakes. Especially heavy traffic moved between Cleveland and Detroit, and Cleveland and Buffalo. (Cleveland Press Collection/ CSU Archives)

Passengers boarding at the 9th Street Dock in Cleveland before 1930. (Cleveland Press Collection/CSU Archives)

This McMyler Unloader operating in 1910 was one step in the advance of materials handling. The clamshells lowered into the holds, took a bite, rose to the crane height, traveled over the hopper cars, and released.

The penultimate advance in unloading was the Hulett unloader that, in various models, dominated until the self-unloading vessels became numerous. The Hulett could unload a vessel in four or five hours as opposed to the four or five days of the wheelbarrow era. (Cleveland Press Collection/CSU Archives)

The burning of the *City of Buffalo* on March 22, 1938, at her 9th Street Pier berth stunned the crowd that always came to watch her arrivals and departures. It also stunned the famous half-century-old Cleveland & Buffalo Transit Company. Already faltering from low-traffic depression years, the company was pushed over the edge by the burning of this great ship.

A porthole view of the Cuyahoga, which has twenty-one bridges spanning its navigable six miles. Good communication signals between vessel and bridge tenders on the lift, swing, and drawbridges are critical. A boat carrying a 20,000-ton load has overwhelming momentum at any speed, so timing of the bridge opening is crucial. (Cleveland Press Collection/CSU Archives)

The 150-ton crane welded to the deck of the *Martha Endeavour* works here in tandem with the ship's 160-ton boom to load this 206-ton casting from the dock to the hold.

Containers being discharged from the *Manchester City*, 1965. Containerization brought enormous efficiencies. Arriving containers could be loaded directly onto trucks at shipside and driven to the consignee without rehandling the individual items in the container—the philosophy of the six pack versus individual cans.

The harbor must be dredged periodically to sustain 27-foot depth. To hold the dredging spoil, the Corps of Engineers is building dikes here in September 1967, using stone hauled in by the self-unloading carrier in the background. (Cleveland Press Collection/ CSU Archives)

First lift for the big crane was this Cleveland-built armored vehicle for shipment to troops in Germany in 1963. (Cleveland Press Collection/CSU Archives)

On a single day in 1970, the Port hosts ships from Sweden (1), Canada (2), Germany (3, 5), Japan (4, 6), Holland (7, 9), and Italy (8). (Cleveland Press Collection/CSU Archives)

With the opening of the St. Lawrence Seaway, Canadian steamers back-hauled "Seaway ore" from Sept Isles on their way upstream to the head of the Lakes for grain cargoes. Here, the Canadian *Scott Misener Royalton* is unloading at Cleveland's C&P Dock in 1969 under the giant Hulett unloaders. (Courtesy of Alan W. Sweigert)

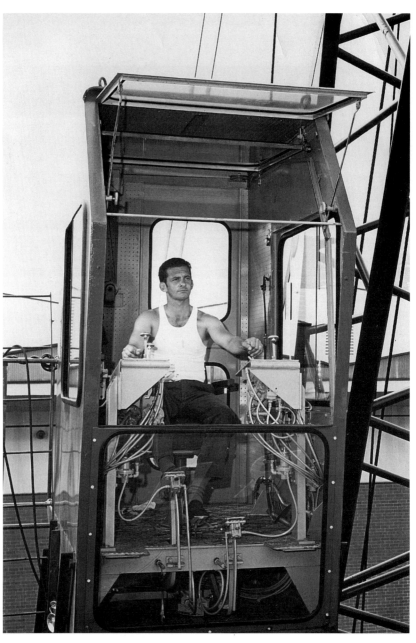

From his cab the crane operator can see both the load and his signalman.

days for the month of October to carry steel coils to Windsor.

Negotiations began for a floating dry dock. The Port and Consolidated Rail Corporation began planning for a container facility. Lykes Line, after a two-year absence, stopped at the Port to load nine gigantic Euclid trucks bound for Yugoslavia.

The Authority resumed a concerted effort to have RTA railcars shipped through the Port. "The Cleveland Cuyahoga–County Port Authority is willing to do anything," the director said to RTA executives, "to get these railcars to move through the Port of Cleveland." The Port was successful in getting seven cars from Italy, which arrived September 1 aboard the *Jean Lykes*. Later in the year, ninety-six light railcars for the Shaker Rapid were scheduled to be shipped through Baltimore, but last-minute lobbying diverted seventeen to Cleveland. Negotiations continued into 1983 and would be a major issue for the new executive director.

While shipbuilding was grinding to a halt in 1981, Republic Steel Corporation christened a new addition to its fleet—the 635-foot ore carrier *American Republic*, built specifically for the Cuyahoga River and general hauling.

Cooperation between the Port and the stevedore companies was critical. The Authority decided to waive storage charges on bulk commodities up to $19,000 to assist the Cleveland Ste-vedore Company in the purchase of two buckets for handling bulk commodities in the Port.

A Big Blow

The Seaway announced a 30-percent increase in tolls over the next two years. This would devastate the Port of Cleveland, and Board members suggested many counterstrategies. They met with senators and congressmen, and sent letters prior to the public hearing scheduled for October. They also unanimously passed Resolution No. 1981-28 formally opposing the increase.

The Board also opposed other damaging federal regulations, particularly the Abdnor-Moynihan Bill and user fees. It sent protest letters to senators and congressmen and Governor Rhodes: "Seaway tolls are detrimental and any legislation regarding user fees should not be acted upon until after the Seaway tolls are matched by every Port in the United States. Charges should be levied and collected on a universal national basis."

The year 1981 saw more lease negotiations. The Port was behind on lease payments to the city because it had invested the money in the bond market and needed to hold the investment through year-end for maximum benefit. The city was displeased; while the Port was earning interest money, the city was losing it.

This and other negotiations, all affected by rising steel imports and high interest rates, would carry over to the new executive director. C. Thomas Burke needed strong shoulders and strong help for the job awaiting him in 1982.

The new chairman, Jay Ehle, had served the Port since 1974 as Board secretary, member of the finance committee, and chairman of the key operations and personnel committee. "I began my maritime career as dock hand; joined Cleveland Builders Supply in 1938 and, after serving in World War II, returned to CBS. I became vice president of operations in 1953, vice president and general manager in 1958, president and CEO in 1963, and president and chairman in 1966. After retiring in 1985, I remained on the CBS board until 1989." The new executive director would face a challenging first year, which included renewal of the levy already receiving opposition from within his own Board.

12

Looking for Work, 1982–1984

"Get Out of the Office"

The Port's new executive director, C. Thomas Burke, charged into the job. His priority was marketing. Vigorous and bold, his modus operandi was "get out of the office" and talk to potential customers.

He first made the rounds of existing Port customers to thank them for their business and hold them for next year. He then moved out to new prospects in Cleveland, then deep into the Port's hinterland, as far inland as St. Louis and Kansas City.

His first ninety days of sales calls were at "full ahead," and along with his staff, he accepted every speaking engagement to advance Port awareness. Burke developed seminars and trade fairs to place the Port in the business community's consciousness.

Railcars Again

Burke and Kenneth Loeri, sales vice president of Cleveland Stevedore, tried to make RTA feel guilty if it could not force Mitsui to ship its order of Japanese-built railcars through Cleveland's Port instead of Philadelphia. "I'd hate to think," Loeri said for publication, "about having unemployed longshoremen out on the street in two years if these cars don't come through our port."

Both RTA and Mitsui were trying to figure out how to use the Cleveland Port, but shipping through

Cleveland's Port would add $20,000 per car.

Burke argued that RTA should pay the extra $1.2 million to help the Cleveland job picture. But as a knowledgeable man with legal training he knew full well that, when federal dollars are even partially involved, any side agreements that artificially increase cost must be paid with local funds.

There were other reasons: federal funding required that the cargo must move on American flag vessels, and at that time there were none *regularly* serving the Great Lakes, and during the winter months none at all.

Many charged that this was just an excuse—that Mitsui had made a "sweet deal" with Philadelphia.

Best of Enemies

The Port was constantly caught between its friends and its friends. Promoting foreign steel imports helped the Port but infuriated local steel producers who were also Port customers and who had supported the Port's creation and its levies.

The city's expressed interest in a lakefront theme park also inspired mixed feelings at the Port. A theme park can use several locations; a port can only use the waterfront. Yet periodically this idea for a citizen entertainment area on the lakefront would resurface with different auspices.

The maritime community was regularly caught between nostalgia and business. For example, the historic, fondly remembered excursion boat *Canadiana* arrived in the Cuyahoga to await restoration. She had many fans, but industrial operators were concerned that the *Canadiana*, resting on the bottom after mysteriously sinking, would slide into the channel and disrupt industrial traffic in the river. Spring flooding damaged her further. Lake men feared she would never haul out. The year would end before the vessel was raised.

With the season barely underway, the Authority took a surprise blow. After all the bargaining on the Dock 20 lease agreement, Lake Erie Asphalt filed for bankruptcy on May 17, leaving the Port owed back-rent and no immediate recourse nor paying tenant in sight. Through bankruptcy proceedings, however, Ohio Bulk Transfer assumed the lease and paid the outstanding rent.

"Nobody's Going to Tell Labor"

The Board practically lost the services of director Martin Hughes, who was involved in two controversies. When Hughes was appointed to the Cuyahoga County Board of Elections, William Calfee, who had tangled with Hughes previously, declared that Hughes could not serve on two boards. Hughes disagreed.

Despite intensive media coverage, Hughes did not resign. This gave the Port's political snipers a still larger target.

Additionally, Hughes, as president of Cleveland AFL-CIO, opposed Ohio's redistricting plan backed by Congresspersons Stokes and Oakar. They demanded Hughes retract his opposition. Hughes said, "Nobody's going to tell labor what to do." Both these battles extended over a long period.

Shipping Action

Slightly delayed by an ice jam at Port Colborne, the season's first saltwater ship, the Greek-registered *Katherine,* tied up at Dock 24 on April 23 with 6,000 tons of Spanish fluorspar for Lincoln Electric. The Greek *Vasilis* followed with 10,000 tons of ferromanganese for U.S. Steel in Lorain.

On May 10, 1982, the Yugoslav *Ravni Kotari* arrived with steel. As many as twenty more steel-hauling ships might arrive by June 10 as steel importers tried to beat a possible cutoff date if the Commerce Department were to find unfair foreign subsidy of steel. Cleveland's steel industry was down to half-capacity.

In July, fifty-five International Harvester dump trucks loaded out of the Port for Egypt.

Also in July, the first RO-RO ship arrived, the Danish *Project Americas.* This 430 foot "roll-on, roll-off" stern-loading vessel could roll on huge machines without using cranes. At Cleveland she loaded twelve 150-ton Terex coal haulers for Gulluk, Turkey.

The Yugoslav vessel *Split,* a Cleveland favorite, loaded 1,500 tons of flour for Tangiers, Morocco, under the federal Food for Peace program. Tom Burke, who had been lobbying the government for this cargo, also anticipated an additional 2,000 tons.

Terex shipped twelve monster off-highway trucks through the Port for Turkey.

The navy destroyer USS *William C. Lawe* visited as part of the third annual Days of the Ships Festival organized by the Oxbow Group, comprised of merchants along the river.

Seventy thousand visitors attended the three-day celebration and toured navy and U.S. and Canadian coast guard vessels. There was a nighttime parade of two hundred illuminated pleasure boats and several kinds of water sport shows and dining and dancing.

Visiting vessels of interest to the public in 1984 would include the Malcolm Forbes yacht, *Highlander;* navy destroyer *Edison,* which drew 78,000 people; the waterborne retreat of American presidents, the yacht *Sequoia;* and the topsail sloop *Providence.*

Fighting the Toll Keeper

The maritime community, supported by the northern Ohio congressional representatives, mounted strong opposition to recurrent talk of Seaway user fees. The Port also pushed the move to forgive the Seaway debt repayment and to halt Seaway tolls or at least to enforce a moratorium on increases.

Tom Burke raised some eyebrows from the podium at the Propeller Club's annual event. "Cleveland–Cuyahoga County Port will oppose any user charges until the matter of our already existing overcharge toll is rectified equitably. In fact we suggest a moratorium on any increase in tolls."

A Senate bill proposed forgiving the U.S. share of the Seaway debt repayment, $110 million. Senator John Glenn played a key role in pushing it through the Senate and Representative Mary Rose Oakar through the House. Before the maritime cheering died out, the Seaway Corporation announced that the dramatic giveback would not forestall raises in Seaway tolls. Funds were needed for extensive repairs.

The Port's 1982 closed adequately but was a disappointment to Tom Burke. "I had no idea how tough it would be."

Turnaround and Turmoil

Just as it announced that the Port would be an official weighing and inspection station for the city, the saga of the Parcel Post Annex again made news, a story that would surface time and again in 1983.

The Park Corporation was still trying to develop the Foreign Free Trade Zone and lease the Post Annex, but progress was slow.

When the U.S. Postal Service finally vacated the building, the Port needed a settlement of $48,900 to compensate for damage to the building.

Arnold Pinkney presented to the Board Joseph A. LoConti of LoConti Management Company as his recommended tenant to develop the building. The plan: $300,000 rent for the first year plus 2.5 percent of gross receipts after ten years on a thirty-year lease. Operations must include a food service and a Free Trade Zone.

In April, LoConti announced that he had a new partner, Gilbert I. Singerman. The Port's counsel, William Calfee, recommended rejecting LoConti's lease, but after deleting some items, the Board approved the lease with only the usual one nay. LoConti and Singerman, now operating under the name 1000 West 9th Street Corporation, opened a small office in the building and hired an architect and engineer to design their $10-million plan for a Food Service

Mart and Foreign Free Trade Zone.

While these plans were developed, the company gave permission for Kassouf Parking Company, manager of the city's impound lot, to use the building's interior and grounds for storing automobiles. Shortly, cars overran the property and payments by Kassouf fell behind. Newspapers ran photos that made Port property look like an auto junkyard. Board members were troubled.

In November, 1000 West 9th Street Corporation told the Board that its financing would be delayed at least six months; in January, the Port informed the corporation that failure to complete payment and improvements by May 31, 1984, would terminate the lease.

As June rolled in and the lease was broken, the corporation asked for compensation for their substantial investment in the structure. Claims and counterclaims continued.

The Port listed the Parcel Post Annex as a fixed asset valued at $4,703,483.25; but it was having trouble marketing this investment.

Upon the expiration of the terms of Bernstein and Hughes, two new members joined the Board in 1983. The mayor appointed John J. (Jack) Dwyer, vice chairman of Oglebay Norton, operator of the Columbia Fleet, thus adding maritime experience to the Board. Dwyer was formerly a Cleveland Heights councilman, chairman of the Cuyahoga-

Lake County Republican Finance Committee, and chairman of the Growth Association in 1980. The county appointed local developer-contractor and lawyer Minor H. George. A former councilman in the southwestern Cleveland suburb of Parma, George had chaired many civic and trade organizations and was well known for his leadership in the local Arab community.

Officers for 1983 were Jay Ehle, chairman and CEO; Campbell Elliott, vice chairman; and Arnold Pinkney, secretary.

The executive director and chairman were an interesting team. Tom Burke's motions were as quick as his enthusiasms and disappointments, both of which were very visible. Ehle, by contrast, was described in a *Plain Dealer* editorial as "very tall even with a severely close cropped brush cut, was equally bold, but his motion and speech were deliberate and his opinions not on the surface. Experience tempered his enthusiasms and his disappointments. He rode an even keel."

Executive Director Burke's efforts to generate more grain and flour exports were starting to pay off; work on eliminating Seaway tolls continued; and the Port pressured for removal of the *Canadiana* from Collision Bend. To hold business, the Board lowered the bulk rate from 40 to 35 cents per ton up to 800,000 tons.

Director Stefan Deubel requested reimbursement for his most recent Romanian trip. While the Board had subsidized one of Deubel's previous European visits, the directors now insisted that trips must be presented and approved prior to the trip. Deubel was not happy.

C. E. Cast, the tenant in Warehouse A, notified the Port of its intent to terminate its lease. It offered to remain until another tenant could be found, or until the lease expired, but by July the warehouse was vacant.

Coakley Terminals's new stripping, stuffing, and container repair service became operational in August and by year end reported eight hundred containers had passed through its facility.

In early summer, the Great Lakes Governors Conference met in Cleveland to consider a common market strategy for economic revitalization. A reception held aboard the American Steamship Company's *American Republic* hosted a distinguished company, including Governors Robert Orr of Indiana, Anthony Earl of Wisconsin, James Blanchard of Michigan, and Richard Celeste of Ohio.

Calling at Cleveland

April brought the first ship of 1983, Liberian-registered *Stolt Sydness,* but her arrival marked the first time in seventy-two years that the season's first ship arrived empty. The tanker loaded 1,300 tons of liquid latex manufactured at General Tire & Rubber in Akron bound for Belgium.

The MV *Yeral* arrived from Conakry, Africa, with a sixteen-year-old stowaway aboard. The captain's repeated attempts to arrange Selson Camara's return to Guinea were blocked by stringent U.S. customs laws. After the ship reached a Canadian port, the boy was on his way home with a full suitcase and a $5,000 education fund.

The Port had another unusual visitor this year, a replica of a Viking dragon ship. The seventy-six-foot vessel arrived aboard the Norwegian freighter *Brunto* in late summer. Minnesota resident Robert Asp had worked ten years on this ship. Following his death, Asp's family helped sail the ship to Norway. The ship was returning to Minnesota to be the centerpiece of a learning center.

Taking Stock

The annual independent audit of the Port stirred wide interest. The city's plans for lakefront development initially included a new aquarium, marine museum, and park. To remain on track, it requested an early return on the Port's 1982 audit. Chairman Ehle's job proliferated. He also served on the city's Waterfront Advisory Committee and was aware that the city was considering taking property now leased to the Port as the site for these entertainment developments.

The city's plans did not please the Port, and their request for a 300-percent rent increase (to $1,200,000) stunned the Board. The city offered an alternate proposal: If the Port would give up Dock 32 to the city for recreational purposes (and perhaps Docks 28, 29, and 30), the rent would be raised only 30 percent.

While the city owned the land and could legally take it away, that would adversely affect the Port's business and the $1 billion that shipping annually pumped into the community. Dock 32 was the Port's busiest dock, especially for steel shipments; and its safest dock in a storm. Moved to another dock, the business could not be handled with the same efficiency.

John Baker, newly elected president of the Great Lakes district of the ILA, again suggested the Port buy the docks from the city and end all the interference. This received continued attention, and in September the directors discussed moving to Whiskey Island if and when the city reclaimed its docks.

Late in the month, the Corps of Engineers announced its plan for extending the shipping season to a full twelve months. But the $6-billion price tag discouraged some of the plan's earliest backers.

Great Lakes Towing dedicated its new $700,000 steel floating dry dock at its Division Avenue shipyard on the Cuyahoga. The *Favorite* was the largest dry dock on Lake Erie specifically designed for commercial small craft, including tugboats and other floating equipment.

While the Seaway's single biggest cargo was grain, 80 percent of the Port's cargo in 1983 was steel and ore. The Port did receive its single largest allocation from the USDA: five million pounds of flour, destined for Egypt and Peru, part of the government's Food for Peace Program (called "PL480 cargo").

Despite consistent efforts by Burke and the Board to bring the RTA's Japanese deliveries through the Port of Cleveland, including strong editorials in the *Plain Dealer,* the cars were delivered to the Seattle port, eventually arriving in Cleveland—*by rail*—for final assembly.

Both Ford and General Motors applied for and received Foreign Free Trade Subzones. But new federal regulations prevented the Port from making any money on subzones, and even the $25,000 a year the Port had garnered from the Park Corporation was now reduced to a charge of $10,000, the standard for any subzone. The only benefit to the Port would be the possibility of cargo for the docks en route to the zone.

The Big Meeting

In anticipation of a major announcement, the November 9 meeting was packed with television cameras and over fifty spectators (including the new head of the Cleveland Stevedore Company, Thomas F. Coakley, Jr.).

The Port detailed plans for lengthening Dock 26 to accommodate three ships and for the construction of more warehouses at a combined cost of $25 million. This was news.

In addition, labor and the stevedoring companies used this forum to severely criticize the city's plan to reclaim the docks. There were alternate suggestions for placement of the city's recreational facilities and more discussion concerning Whiskey Island.

The Port's business at year-end boomed, and projections for 1984 were optimistic. The year's 53-percent increase in general cargo was due in great part to PL480 shipments of agricultural products for disaster relief or other humanitarian purposes. These shipments were mostly grain in hundred-pound bags. News that PL480 cargoes would be diverted from the Great Lakes to tidewater ports prompted thirteen senators, including Ohio's Glenn and Metzenbaum, to write protests to the USDA.

Final statistics for 1983 showed 655,566 tons handled plus 464,427 tons of ore pellets lightered in Cleveland. The Port had not handled so much international cargo since 1977. New bulk commodities to the Port were iron ore briquettes from Venezuela and pig iron from Brazil. This

positive business turnaround enabled the Port to pay the final installment on $5.7 million in bonds and notes from the Port's first bond issue. Attorney Calfee told the *Plain Dealer*, "It was like burning a mortgage!"

On December 8, the 240th and last ship of the season unloaded.

The Board received a congratulatory letter from Governor Celeste. Ehle received a special commendation from the Ohio State General Assembly. It looked as though the Port of Cleveland might have reason to celebrate as the twenty-fifth anniversary of the Seaway approached.

With the tax anticipation notes paid, the Port delivered $400,000 in rent to the city. The chairman appointed Campbell Elliott, Jack Dwyer, and Minor George to a special committee to oversee the continuing lease negotiations. The Port hired Anthony Russo, former deputy director of the Port, as a special consultant. Two new men joined the Board. Carmen E. Parise, secretary-treasurer and business representative of Newspaper Drivers Local 473, was appointed by the county commissioners upon the expired term of Sheldon Schecter. The Reverend Sterling E. Glover replaced Reverend Otis Moss. Glover came to Cleveland in 1966 from Scotch Plains, New Jersey, to serve as pastor of Emmanuel Baptist Church. Prior to his Port appointment, Glover assisted in the formation of the Ministerial Day Care Association, Emmanuel Family Training Center, Inc., the Langston Hughes Center, and the Booker/Sterling Preparatory School.

Special-events parking on the working docks was hotly debated. Several companies were interested in bidding and sent representatives to the March 1984 Board meeting. Some members felt that the financial bid need not be the real issue but rather business reputation and financial responsibility. The matter was handed to the operations committee for study; it invited proposals before March 15.

But the problem resurfaced with verbal attacks, threatened law suits, and accusations. The chairman extended the deadline: all sealed bids to be submitted by April 11, 1984, contract awarded to highest bidder. It turned out to be Kassouf at $60,000.

Late in April, on this twenty-fifth-anniversary year of the Seaway, a mammoth ice jam in the St. Clair River backed up ships and water in the Great Lakes for almost three weeks. It required eight ice breakers to finally clear passage. While the shipping impact was immediate and dramatic, with loss estimates placed at $1.5 million a day, the affect on Great Lakes water levels would be long term.

When the old Coast Guard Station was again introduced, the Board passed a resolution to acquire the space from General Service Administration, which was eager to transfer it. The State of Ohio, however, took a different view, and eventually the Port returned 1,393 acres of submerged land under the abandoned facility to the state, which made it possible for the state to sell the station.

Gary Welsh, an investigative reporter for the *Plain Dealer*, started showing up at meetings. On April 27 he questioned Arnold Pinkney about a conflict of interest. Under the editorial headline "The Aroma of Special Deals," the *Plain Dealer:* "Besides arranging a favorable lease of the old post office annex for a business associate, and then selling him insurance, Pinkney also sold insurance policies to Port Authority board members. His colleagues agreed to place Authority funds in a bank where he is an officer, an investment that cost the port thousands of dollars in interest earnings."

To make matters worse, Pinkney had been head of the search committee that located and recommended Burke for the executive director's job. During a bonding process, it was discovered that Burke had not been forthcoming about a bankruptcy claim on his application. Investigation revealed a well-marked trail of financial problems that followed Burke from Duluth to Cleveland.

The Port had its first-ever ocean-going barge shipment when Terex shipped seventeen large earth-moving units (worth $6.5 million). The barge was routed through the Great Lakes to Chicago and then towed down the Calumet River to the Mississippi River and on to New Orleans and then South America.

In the ongoing lease negotiation with the city, the chairman was authorized to enter a seven-year lease for Docks 24, 26, 28, 30, and 32. Although the rent increased only $100,000 (to $500,000), there was a cancellation clause: the city could negate for recreational or commercial development purposes with two-years' notice.

Thus began the tug of war for the Port's very existence.

Dock 20 was in dispute again with questions about a $22,500 payment from Ohio Bulk Transfer for winter ore storage. Prompted by a misunderstanding with Jones & Laughlin, the Board authorized the executive director to negotiate, but the discussion would not be settled until October, with Ohio Bulk Transfer agreeing to pay half the amount.

The June 18 special meeting to designate depositories was far from routine this year because some Board members were also serving as directors of banks. Conflict of interest hung in the air.

As summer depleted the ranks of the Board, the budget hearing committee met in the hospital room of Campbell Elliott to achieve a quorum.

In October, Jones & Laughlin merged with Republic Steel, abandoning Dock 20 for the Lorain docks. This was particularly bad news when coupled with termination of rents from Warehouse A and the Parcel Post Building. Only wharfage and dockage were up.

Kassouf and Company was now in default on their parking contract, and the Port signed a new $30,000-plus percentage agreement with Ameripark.

LoConti/Singerman's corporation was also in default on the Parcel Post building. The Board, while hoping for $300,000–$600,000, agreed to a settlement of $60,000. Pinkney abstained.

But despite difficulties, skyrocketing imports coupled with the overvalued dollar and a general economic recovery clogged East Coast ports with foreign goods in 1984. This caused Cleveland shippers, who had come to favor Eastern ports, to take renewed interest in their hometown port.

Then, just as shipping was about to close for the year, a major bridge broke down and stranded 160 ships in the Seaway for almost three weeks. The commission lengthened the season to December 31.

This breakdown also boosted business at Cleveland's Port. When the bridge was finally repaired and traffic resumed on December 10, some ships—uncertain that they could reach their destination and return before the waterway closed for the season—unloaded at Cleveland rather than risk the long trip to the northern Lake ports.

The overall cargo moving in and out of the Port (1,378,000 tons) was up more than 23 percent, making 1984 the second best year in the Port Authority's sixteen-year history and the first year that the Cleveland–Cuyahoga County Port Authority operated a full year debt free.

13

The Agent

Dennis Mahoney here. . . . No, Hugh's down at the dock. Can I help you?

Well she's just docking now as we're speaking and I just talked to Hugh and he's . . . certainly she's not getting out today. Very possibly tomorrow. But late. That's earliest possibility. And we haven't received official word yet on whether or not she'll do a top off outside the river because of the draft. That's current info, maybe ten minutes ago.

One of the several frenetic nerve centers of the Lakes is the office of lanky Dennis "Doc" Mahoney of World Shipping, Inc.

Ships move slowly, and because they do, they throw their shore support periodically into feverish action preparing for their arrival, discharging, loading, and departure. Since the vessel's operating cost may be $15,000 to $20,000 a day, everyone scrambles to eliminate idle time at the dock, to keep the ships moving.

Ever since ships sailed far from home, they have needed a friend in their distant ports of call. With the arrival of steam and diesel and governmental involvement, this little-known friend became even more essential. He is the ship's agent.

The agent procures cargo for the ship, arranges for ship's supplies, arranges for ship chandlers and repairs and provisioning. He arranges for doctors or lawyers and liaison between the ship and shippers, consignees, local Customs, and other government bodies.

Today a ship's agent may be a very large company, such as World Shipping, but the function is the same.

While World Shipping is a large corporation with three divisions, Doc Mahoney's "war room"—complete with desk, extra chair, filing cabinet, small table, computer, two Great Lakes wall maps—wraps around him like oil skins. Dressed in casuals, ready for a run to the docks, but with precision-groomed, prematurely graying hair, Mahoney operates this cockpit with the deep relaxed drawl of a man who knows exactly what he's doing, where his ships are, and what everyone else involved will be doing about them, for them, and around them. His long reach sweeps some layers of paper aside to open up space for a visitor's coffee cup. His long reach across the Lakes is logged on a legal pad on his desk that documents marine events from the viewpoint of his office.

And from Mahoney's office, even if a visitor does not understand all the in-house idioms, a radarlike map of maritime action in a hundred-mile radius unfolds as Mahoney coordinates his client ships with stevedores, Customs, Coast Guard, consignees, immigration, USDA, linesmen, surveyors, ship chandlers, and suppliers.

A slot in Mahoney's wall is a pass-through window to his colleague Hugh Goldie. Goldie is considered the dean of the ships agentry indus-try. He has been with World Shipping for twenty-eight years. At this moment, he is phoning Mahoney on a cellular phone from the dock, asking for some information.

Mahoney responds, "No, Hugh, the visa crew list has not arrived yet. Is the ship there? . . . Okay. . . . Two tugs—one? . . . Okay. What time's Immigration coming down? . . . So they're probably already standing down there waiting . . . . Not yet? Okay. . . . Is this visa supposed to come in via courier, Hugh?"

To the visitor, Mahoney then explains about a ship arriving tomorrow. "People will be calling in for information because they all have to coordinate their activities. We're the ones who coordinate and advise. For instance this morning, [there] is a Fed Nav vessel out of Montreal—I sent them this message to advise them of the present and projected weather here."

Mahoney shows the visitor a fax of expected weather conditions. In the middle, large block letters warn "STRONG POSSIBILITY RAIN SATURDAY."

The vessel's arrival had been delayed by a pilot shortage followed by the thirty-seven-hour lift up 326 feet via eight locks at the Welland Canal.

Later Mahoney explained, "I need to talk to our office in Detroit because they're going to be the agents for the vessel's next port, which will be Toledo. They're only fifty-five miles from Toledo, and the steve-dores in Toledo want to make their plans. Now we know that Toledo doesn't have to worry about the weekend. We plan to work this ship with just enough gangs for just enough time that we can complete on Monday. We minimize our over-time—we set a goal. What we want to achieve is a Monday night finish, and we know what that goal is going to cost with our overtime on Sunday. In this case we'll be spending over five thousand dollars in overtime to en-able us to complete the ship on Mon-day. But the ship's value is $10,000 to $15,000 a day to the ship operator. They're renting the vessel on long-term time-charter, paying roughly $15,000 a day. So you want to keep the ship moving, generally speaking; but you don't want to throw money away on overtime.

"For example, tomorrow there's a high probability of rain; the ship can't start first thing in the morning any-how. If we wanted to finish on Sun-day we'd have to work a long day on Saturday with a high risk of rain and still work Sunday; and we'd be spending about twice as much in overtime and probably end up get-ting rained out and paying stand-by time to the stevedore. Stand-by is even more expensive than overtime. So those are some of the risks we weighed in making the decisions."

"You can't unload in the rain?"

"Certain cargoes—yes. But cold rolled steel products are definitely rain sensitive, and that's what this ship is carrying."

Mahoney takes a call from his World Shipping colleague, Bob Audy, on a mobile phone in Detroit. "Bob, What can I do for you? . . . You mean the *Lake Champlain,* yes I did indeed and she is going to . . . we've decided she'll work Sunday in Cleveland, just enough OT to finish Monday night. You'll have her in Toledo on Tuesday morning. You're on a mobile, aren't you? . . . Yeah, I've got to call Steve and let him know as well. Might have to take care . . . . Which? For the *Champlain?* . . . Well, okay. She's not going to dock before then. . . . Okay, that's cool. I can take care of Toledo. We'll keep in touch particularly on Monday. Could you courier the file to me?"

The visitor asked, "What is he go-ing to courier?"

"The file for the ship. They're go-ing to be too busy up in Detroit to physically be in attendance when this same ship that we have coming into Cleveland arrives [at] Toledo. Looks like they're going to be jammed up. So I'll go to Toledo. We cover for each other. You can't be sufficiently staffed for the busy season; you'd have to lay off too many people in off season. So in peak periods we work around the clock with the same people. There seems to be an early demand for steel in Detroit this season. Ships from Europe, Brazil, Russia . . . former

Soviet block countries in need of money have raw steel products to sell and a lot of aluminum."

Mahoney makes a call to the stevedore company. "Chris? Doc. Here's our new plan, sir. Work two gangs on Sunday, eight hours each. Three gangs on Monday 0800. I assume you don't want to change berths . . . you still want to do 26 west . . . after the *Solpinas* sails . . . what time is she due to sail? She's got five hours work . . . and she's starting at 0800 tomorrow? All right so we'll have to coordinate this accordingly so she'll sail . . . maybe you'll do a meal period, maybe going to bring a gang back, one of those . . . we'll have to kinda watch that.

"Well she's going to be out there say about noon anyhow . . . I'll bring her in *immediately* upon . . . as soon as the *Solpinas* clears the harbor. We'd like to touch in all three of those hatches. You know, because we've got a nine hour and a seventeen, a nine and a fourteen hour hatch."

Mahoney takes a call. "Letter in the mail? Oh! About dangerous cargo. Oh yeah that's in the post. Everything you'll want to know about dangerous cargo is in that."

Mahoney summed up the agent's job, "Making sure that ev-ree-thing that needs to be done with these ships is done, that there are no preventable delays . . . that the crew matters are all taken care of . . . that they're healthy . . . the cargo is okay . . . the

paperwork formalities . . . all the manifest corrections . . . freight corrections . . . cargo releases . . . anything that's got to do with that ship, its cargo, the people. We have to protect the interests of our principals and if we didn't do an adequate job, they'd find somebody that does."

That challenge long ago created this fascinating profession. The ship agent may be one person or a large staff or several offices in several ports.

Preparing in advance for the ship's arrival and departure, the agent's most important chore is lining up cargoes. He is the ship's salesman. In that role, the agent is working for both the vessel company and for the shipper of the cargo.

Mahoney has alerted Immigration and Customs so that they can arrive promptly and not delay the unloading. Nothing is unloaded until Immigration comes aboard to verify the crew and Customs checks the cargo against the manifests.

All of this requires yards of paper documentation. Doc has this ready for signing so the longshoremen can be signaled that it's okay to board.

Dennis Mahoney will see to all the needs of the ship and crew while she's in port.

How This Agency Was Born

In Lorain, Ohio, a port city, a shipbuilding city, and home to a lot of

Great Lakes maritime families, young Jack Hunger had a grandfather and a father who were chief engineers on Great Lakes ore boats. Jack rode the boats in the summers, learning the Great Lakes, its cities, its ports, and its docks. Upon graduation from Lorain High, Jack went to Ohio State, where he joined the Navy Reserve Officer Training Program. There he learned about the Merchant Marine Academy, King's Point, which he attended and graduated from with a B.S. in marine transportation and as an ensign in the U.S. Naval Reserve.

That was in 1957, just as the Seaway was about to open the Great Lakes to world shipping. Jack Hunger saw opportunity. After brief navy active duty, he joined Grace Lines in New York as a ship's officer and later moved ashore into management.

Grace was beginning a service from the Great Lakes to the Caribbean. The line sent Jack to Chicago to operate their ships. After a year, Grace decided to abandon its Great Lakes service and bring Jack back to New York.

However, Jack declined.

He went to Cleveland instead and hung out his own shingle in the Standard Building as ships agent, modestly lettered: "World Shipping, Inc."

He launched his business amid twenty experienced steamship agencies in Cleveland, all seeking to represent many new ocean lines coming into the Lakes from northern Europe, the Mediterranean, the Caribbean, and the Far East.

In the "good 1960s" the agents flourished as about thirty ship lines came up the Seaway, most notably Fjell-Orange, Hapag-Lloyd, Manchester, Salvesen, and Mitsui OSK.

Hunger began making calls. His timing was good, and on this rising tide of world trade in the Lakes he built solid relationships with ship owners, shippers, stevedore companies, and the complex of involved government agencies. His early vessel accounts were Nordlake Line, Salvesen, and Hellenic.

Hunger also became agent for tramp ships handling largely cargoes of steel and ores and bulk liquid. (Liquid cargoes tended to be oil, tallow, vegetable oils, and asphalt. Some came in sophisticated tankers, others on regular ships in drums.)

"Tramp ship" is not a negative phrase. It may be the more romantic part of the business. A tramp is a kind of free-lance ship picking up cargoes wherever it finds them. It is usually operated by a small group of owners, sometimes just the captain and his family. The vessels tend to be smaller, however, some are very sophisticated. A tramp ship especially depends on the agent for its cargoes.

Hunger's knowledge of the Lakes ports and exporters and his dedication and energy plus the escalating market of the 1960s propelled his agency rapidly. It was soon arranging cargoes and vessel needs at Lake Erie ports from Buffalo to Detroit.

Hunger knew the good work of Sam Ricciardi, whom he asked to join World Shipping in 1965, offering shares in the company. In a business relationship that endured for decades, the two men rapidly added more and more customers, requiring, of course, more staff. Very early the company opened offices in Detroit, Rochester, Pittsburgh, Cincinnati, and Chicago.

Soon the young agency was handling work for heartland exporters using ocean coastal ports instead of only the Seaway, which was closed in winter.

Radical Sea Change

That new focus proved pivotal in the company's destiny, because a sweeping change, as radical as the change from sail to diesel, was swiftly revolutionizing ocean transport: containerization.

Containers are 20- and 40-foot-long metal boxes (like truck trailers without wheels) that can be railroaded to the ports on flat cars and hoisted directly aboard ship. Handled by huge cranes and giant lift trucks, containers did not require large longshoremen gangs. Also, containerized cargoes were protected against damage, pilferage, and weather. Some shippers have less-

than-container loads (LCL). Several such loads headed for the same port can be combined in one container, then broken down at the destination port and distributed to separate consignees by truck or rail.

This new wave came on as swiftly as the railroad piggy-back innovation and it changed the action at every port. It changed the loading tools; it changed the design of ships. More important to this story, it changed the flow of general cargoes away from Great Lakes ports.

Why? Beyond closed winter shipping season was another roadblock to Great Lakes agents, a deal made in the 1950s to achieve Seaway enabling legislation. Powerful Eastern and Gulf port legislators agreed to vote for the Seaway *only* if built to limit passage by vessels no longer that 730 feet.

However, the most efficient use of containers was to load thousands of containers aboard a single ship. That meant using larger ships, too large for Seaway transit. At this writing container ships are over a thousand feet long and a hundred feet wide and carry four thousand containers. On the drawing boards is a new generation of ships that will carry five thousand containers.

Very rapidly, as the 1970s opened, the twenty ship agencies in Cleveland disappeared as container shippers diverted cargoes to the Gulf and coastal ports.

World Shipping, Inc., however, made opportunity out of what other agencies saw as reason to close. Hunger recalls, "Containerization meant enormous new capital expenditures for the shipping lines. It became imperative for them to develop reliable control over their huge fleets of containers when their boxes were scattered all over the world."

Hence World Shipping created a subsidiary, Rail Container Services, Inc. An inland container depot, Rail Container gave shipping companies a central location to gather their inbound containers once they were emptied. Rail Container inspected the containers, reported their condition to the owners, provided storage until next use, and, if authorized, managed repair of damaged containers.

This business grew so rapidly that the subsidiary established depots in six cities. Annually, thousands of containers flow through these depots. The company serves over a hundred major container shipping lines and container leasing companies.

Containerization led World Shipping to another big step in 1973, creation of Midwest Container Services, Inc. The mission was to help Midwest exporters move their container cargoes to the ports, directly to shipside, by rail or truck. This service grew so that the company established a network of inland terminals strategically located in Midwest cities. In 1986 Rail Container and Midwest Container merged to become Container Port Group, Inc.

Today the company lives up to the name Jack Hunger put on his first office door, World Shipping.

Some 130 ship agent companies in the U.S. are members of the Association of Ship Brokers and Agents. An indication of how World Shipping stands in its industry is the fact that Hunger served as president of the association in 1985–86.

Despite World Shipping's international business, it is still the largest customer of the Port in Cleveland because it services and finds cargoes for the charter and tramp vessels using the Port. The company takes full care of the ship as it approaches, while it's here, and as it leaves.

After the *Lake Champlain* is loaded, Hugh Goldie and Doc Mahoney will see that all crew are safely back aboard, line handlers are available, and the ship's next port is notified of her departure.

One of them will be the last man off the ship, "So long, Captain. Good trip to you."

14

The Stevedore

In 1911 Cleveland dedicated the beautiful new Federal Building. John D. Rockefeller walked the center aisle of his church, counting heads to see if there were enough to justify donating $500,000 to build a new church. There were. He built it at East 18th Street. Former mayor Tom L. Johnson died. Cleveland elected Newton D. Baker mayor. That year ore docks, called the largest on the Lakes, were being built on Cleveland's lakefront. The Pennsylvania Railroad hastened construction of a huge plant on the west side basin of the harbor with $3 million worth of bins to hold the cargoes of nearly one hundred ships.

Amid this activity, John Coakley started the Cleveland Stevedore Company.

This is largely the story of the Coakley family and its history in the Port of Cleveland. It is unusual today to find such a continuous commitment to an industry, one still being carried on by the third generation. All the Irish "dock wallopers" of the past who dominated the Gulf Coast stevedoring companies (T. Smith in New Orleans and McGrath Corporation on the East Coast) have either ceased to exist, sold out, or become part of large conglomerates. The Coakleys have always found a way to carry on.

The family's roots are in Pittsburgh, where John A. Coakley, Sr., grew up in the age of "Big Steel," when the fortunes of the family and the Cleveland Stevedore Company paralleled the American steel industry.

By attending night school and working during the day, John graduated with a bachelor of arts degree in 1908 and a law degree in 1912 from Baldwin-Wallace College in Berea, Ohio.

He began his work life in 1892 as an office boy for the Pennsylvania Railroad in Pittsburgh. He went to work for the American Steel Hoop Company in 1898 as chief clerk and in 1904 moved to Cleveland, where he became a division freight agent for the American Steel & Wire Company.

Seeing the rising lake traffic of boats that needed to be loaded and unloaded, Coakley founded the Cleveland Stevedore Company. He did this without leaving his job at American Steel & Wire, where he became vice president of traffic in 1927.

In 1932 he resigned from American Steel & Wire to become general traffic manager for all U.S. Steel Corporation subsidiaries: Carnegie-Illinois Steel Company, National Trade Company, American Steel & Wire Company, American Bridge Company, Columbus Steel Company, H. C. Frick Coke Company, American Sheet and Tinplate Company, and Lorain Steel Company.

Coakley's business interests outside of U.S. Steel began demanding more and more of his time, and in 1937 he resigned from U.S.S. to pursue, full time, management of his nine companies, including the Cleveland Stevedore Company.

From Marcus Hanna's old offices in the Perry Payne Building, he guided growth of his business on a parallel course with the U.S. Great Lakes ore and coal traffic. Cleveland Stevedore Company, in 1937, handled not only package freighters at Docks 20 and 22 in Cleveland, but it also served the steel industries of West Virginia, Ohio, and Pennsylvania through Huron, Ohio, docks. Cleveland, in those years, handled cargoes of cocoa beans to Hershey, Pennsylvania; barbed wire for the West; and steel in all sizes and for every use.

The Small Ships

In the 1940s and 1950s, Great Lakes cargo moved in small ships through the old Seaway and in barges from the East Coast. Small 200-foot Scandinavian ships discharged partial cargoes in Montreal to get to a 14-foot draft and continued on to Cleveland, Detroit, and Chicago. Lakes vessels were carrying import molds from Duluth; structural steel from Lackawanna, New York; pig iron from Quebec; and scrap cargoes loading out of Cleveland for overseas. Between the two World Wars, cargo continued to move through Docks 20 and 22 and Whiskey Island Dock 1.

John A. Coakley, Sr., at the end of World War II, had the foresight to build Riverfront Terminal. Riverfront was located just under the Main Avenue Bridge on the west bank of the

Cuyahoga River on land leased from B&O Railroad. It operated until the sixties, when Seaway vessels became too tall to get under the Conrail railroad bridge south of Dock 20.

Sycamore Dock, also owned by the Cleveland Stevedore Company, was located just south of Riverfront. Sycamore was used by the Stag Line for fluorspar from Spain for Harshaw Chemical, sulfur from Mexico for Grasselli, and liquid tallow loaded into Stolt Tankers for Darling Company. Carbon electrodes from Union Carbide in Tennessee shipped to power stations in Sweden on the Wallenius Line, the line of famous ships named after famous operas.

The Cleveland Stevedore Company was growing steadily in 1946 but the real stimulus to the company's growth arrived in Cleveland courtesy of the U.S. Army Air Corps. Following his military discharge, Captain Thomas F. Coakley arrived at the Cleveland Stevedore Company at exactly the right moment in history, and the company was never again to be the same. Thomas Coakley brought new international perspective to the company and, by the power of his energy and personality, took the company into the new Seaway era and the public eye.

To give T. F. Coakley more complete Lake traffic background, he was first sent to manage the Huron Docks. He returned to Cleveland in 1950 and, following the death of J. A.

Coakley, Sr., in 1955, became president of the Cleveland Stevedore Company.

From the company's conservative, reserved posture, T. F. Coakley moved it into a highly visible position of leadership in U.S. and Great Lakes shipping circles. In 1958 he became national president of the Propeller Club and focused on preparation for the Seaway opening. He traveled the world extensively, developing relationships with many prospective shipping lines that might use the newly built passageway to the "Fourth Coast."

During this period there were four stevedore companies in Cleveland. Cleveland Stevedore began important relationships worldwide that continue to this day, from the little "Potsdam" ships that dropped 100 tons in each port to the huge bulk carriers sailing low in the water.

Coakley planned on the type of docks that would be needed to handle the largest ships able to transit the Seaway and had the good timing to build Dock 26 at the front of West 3rd. Dock 26 was a modern pier in every sense and was a magnet for new business.

Storm Flag

However, there was a dangerous undercurrent threatening Cleveland's waterfront and Cleveland Stevedore's bright future. Managing this crisis would take all of T. F. Coakley's business skill, courage, and good old Irish luck.

The International Longshoremen's Association, born on the Great Lakes in the 1800s, was expelled from the old American Federation of Labor (AFL) for alleged racketeering in 1953. However, the expulsion did not diminish the union's ambitions for organizing all the Great Lakes ports. When the ILA moved out, the International Brotherhood of Longshoremen moved in. It was established by the AFL to replace the ILA. In the early 1950s, the bargaining unit for the Cleveland Stevedore Company and the other waterfront workers was headed by Walter "Wobbly" Weaver, and the hiring of longshoremen was done daily at the company's front gate by the company foreman. Union relationships were cordial, and 20 percent of the men who worked on the waterfront were steady workers and 80 percent casual, *very* casual!

Some of the men working the docks in this period were alcoholics and ex-convicts who worked only until they could get an advance to keep their buzz going at the Flat Iron Cafe, Kindlers, or the Harbor Inn. The company foremen were mostly English, and to understand the language on the piers you had to be able to translate a heavy Liverpool accent.

It was this casual way of hiring that provided the ILA the wedge it needed to gain reentry to the waterfront. Individuals could not get hired until the company had a need for the skills of a particular individual; hence, there was a hiring discipline whereby the company policed drunkenness, theft, and general laziness. The control of this hiring, or "shape-up," would rule the waterfront; and it was this "shape-up" that the ILA used to wrest control away from Wobbly Weaver.

The ILA leader who was to emerge on the Cleveland waterfront during this period was one of the brightest, boldest racketeers in the city's history, Danny Greene. Greene grew up in Collinwood with a strong reputation as a street fighter. The loss of revenue that Cleveland Stevedore Company would incur during Danny Greene's era will probably never be known, but it was millions of dollars. He had supervisors and foremen roughed up and wrecked company equipment, and he even threatened T. F. Coakley and his family. The result was that steamship line after line left Cleveland and went to the relative serenity of Erie, Toledo, and Ashtabula.

Shootings, dynamiting, hijacking, and intimidation became the order of the day, as Danny Greene consolidated his power on the Cleveland waterfront and became the new president of the International Longshoremen's Association, Local 1317.

The Southeast Asian cargoes of

rubber, tin, tapioca, and plywood that Coakley had worked so hard to secure for his new Dock 26 were chased out of Cleveland by a series of strikes, slowdowns, and total chaos that was to give the Port of Cleveland a notoriety from which it took years to recover. The damage Greene inflicted on the Cleveland Stevedore Company nearly destroyed the company's Cleveland operation.

Midnight Meeting

All of this would come to a head in 1961 at the now-famous midnight meeting between T. F. Coakley and Greene. At this meeting, Greene convinced Coakley that the union's control of the hiring hall was needed to bring labor peace to the Cleveland waterfront. The hiring hall, in Greene's eye, was a place where "Irish kids could get a decent day's work for a decent day's pay."

Coakley, who was seeking progress as well as peace and badly needed Greene's cooperation, agreed. What helped him agree, no doubt, was the ongoing strike that idled all of Cleveland Stevedore's docks while its best customers were being handled by a nearby competing dock, Lederer Terminal, not yet affected by the strike. When the strike hit Lederer the following week, it too conceded to the ILA hiring hall.

The hiring hall that emerged in 1962 was not what any of the compa-

nies had ever imagined or agreed to. It was a way for Danny Greene to give the best jobs to his best pals, and anyone who "worked a little too hard" was run off the waterfront or roughed up.

Efficiency and production decreased dramatically, and rubber ships of Ned Lloyd and Orient Mid East who had enjoyed unloading service of thirty tons per hour suddenly found the same cargoes being handled at ten tons per hour. The company losses were astronomical. The cargo went to other ports when the Cleveland Stevedore Company was unable to adjust the rates to cover production losses.

The Port of Cleveland was a combat zone from 1962 to 1965. Danny Greene's motto was "give or take." "The company gives us what we want—or we take it." New stewards appeared daily, direct from jail, and another set of rules went into effect that week.

Coakley Goes Public

T. F. Coakley, when seeing his business in ruin, finally lashed out through a series of newspaper articles.

The *Plain Dealer* uncovered the chaos of the waterfront in a week-long, front-page, award-winning series of articles by Sam Marshall. The ILA in New York finally took notice of the problem in Cleveland and, when it was discovered that men were working grain ships free and Greene was stealing their pay, placed Local 1317 under trusteeship.

In 1965 Chauncey and John Baker were elected to the new union leadership, and to this day they have run the union on a professional basis, restoring relative stability to the Cleveland waterfront. The relationship between the Coakleys and the Bakers, while at times confrontational, is based on mutual respect and the same fierce pride of independence the Irish brought to the waterfront all along the East Coast.

Chauncey and John Baker, at great personal risk, stood up to Danny Greene at the height of his power and today run the union in a quiet, though no less difficult, time. The Cleveland Stevedore Company worked its way out of red ink.

The company, profitable by the end of the 1960s, was again challenged with investing substantial sums of capital for cranes and fork trucks to handle larger ships carrying cargoes of steel and containers that came into Cleveland. Ships from Hamburg-Amerika Line, Nor Deutscher Lloyd, Ernst Russ, Manchester Liners, Swedish-American Line, French Line, Bristol City Line, Federal Commerce and Navigation, and "K" Line established regular services to Cleveland, loading and discharging every type of cargo. Business continued to grow for Cleveland

exporters such as the Eaton Corporation, Lincoln Electric, U.S. Steel, the Higbee Company, Republic Steel, the Midland Ross Corporation, Ferry Cap & Screw, and Cleaner Hangers. Relationships flourished with Wheeling Pittsburgh, Weirton Steel, Sharon Steel, and Allegheny Ludlum as these mills exported steel cargoes to customers around the world via the Cleveland Stevedore docks.

In 1968 the Cleveland–Cuyahoga County Port Authority organized to oversee the entire county and city Port activity, thus ending City Hall's direct influence. However, Cleveland Stevedore Company had sued the City of Cleveland over the delay of placement of the Port's heavy-lift crane and its preferential awarding of pier leases without legal competitive bidding. It was a transitional period for all involved, and the Port, city, and Cleveland Stevedore Company would enter a new era.

The Cleveland Stevedore Company, now with stable waterfront conditions, grew steadily until the death of T. F. Coakley in 1978. The company carried on under the ownership and management of Mrs. T. F. Coakley.

Generation Three

In 1983, a dynamic new leadership began the third generation of Coakley management when T. F. (Chip)

Coakley, Jr., took control of the company and charted a new course.

Chip Coakley graduated from John Carroll University in Cleveland and studied economics at the University of Manchester in England. After serving in Vietnam as an army ports operations officer in DaNang, he joined Kinsman Lines, the Cleveland steamship arm of George Steinbrenner's American Ship Building Company. He went to Seattle to pursue a banking career, becoming head of Citibank's West Coast marine division. Then, in 1983, at the family's request, he returned to Cleveland.

His vision was to use the Cleveland Stevedore Company as the base to build a multinational transportation and manufacturing company. He created Pacific Great Lakes Cor-poration as the vehicle to ensure survival of the core business and to expand by creating new services for the same "old customers" who had supported the company for years. Pacific Great Lakes Corporation, with the Cleveland Stevedore Company as the hub, provides today's customers with fully integrated domestic and international transportation services. The company has developed expertise in transportation management, traffic consultation, vessel chartering, barging, trucking, warehousing, distribution services, and manufacturing. The company continues to maintain its headquarters in the Port of Cleveland, ensuring continuing relationships with long-term shippers into the Port of Cleveland.

15

The Longshoreman

The approaching *Lake Champlain* triggers a chain reaction ashore. Doc Mahoney of World Shipping calls Harry Gray at Cleveland Stevedore. Harry Gray calls Eddy Thorne, steward at ILA Local 1317. He explains the *Champlain*'s cargo and discharge plans and says, "We'll work *Champlain* Sunday, 0800, Dock twenty-six west, two gangs, three hatches. Finish Monday, 1700, with three gangs, straight time. That's the game plan unless—there's some talk she may do a top-off cargo outside the harbor via barge."

They discuss any special skills needed, and Gray adds, "Need four linesmen standing by from 0300 to tie her up."

Eddy Thorne in turn makes the information into a recording for the telephone answering machine. Longshoremen then phone in after 4 P.M. to 781-5207 to see if there is work. The recording tells them there is a ship to work Sunday starting at 0800 and Monday.

At 0700 longshoremen arrive for the shape-up. Based on a rotation plan to spread the work evenly among its 135 members, men are chosen for two gangs on Sunday, three on Monday. If special skills are needed, special men are chosen.

It was not always this neat.

In the world's historically ungentle seaports, men who could carry hundred-pound sacks of grain up schooner gangways all day long did not attend the art museum tea. Worldwide, saloon-centered dock operations grew up, including in Cleveland.

Longshoremen have been pivotal in maritime history, for while a fairly small crew could man even a large four-master, loading or unloading her needed gangs of men, strong and available. To be most available for handling inbound or outbound cargo, workers gathered in a dockside grog shop; and, of course, one could not just occupy a chair there without giving the proprietor some business. Hence, between ships, longshoremen absorbed strong waters, which often led to strong debates about which gang would unload the approaching ship. The rebuttal stage damaged knuckles, teeth, and tavern furniture. Such men were difficult to manage on loading and unloading, giving rise to a brand of longshoreman leadership based on muscle and weapons. The gang boss surrounded himself with a corps of loyal enforcers whom he rewarded in various ways, including preferential pilferage rights. These kings of the docks decided which longshoremen would get work and which would not.

Despite these conditions, as we often find among men in hard, dangerous work, the stevedore was proud of his life. He was necessary.

Prior to the Seaway, Cleveland's waterfront workers were not interested in steady work. They liked the idea of working when they wanted, and they were devoted to the fermented grape. Many were so financially short, the local president explained, that the union or the stevedore company "had to give them a two dollar drag against pay to go eat or drink something."

In that pre-Seaway era, Local 1317 was headed by Wobbly Weaver. Under his presidency, longshoremen had little stature.

Weaver was followed in 1957 by Daniel J. Greene. Greene was positioned by the famed Babe Triscaro who reported to the Milano family. Triscaro was a Golden Gloves flyweight champion who could have been world champion, but he went to work for Mickey Cohen on the West Coast. He came back to Cleveland as business agent for the Teamsters and later headed one of the largest Teamster locals. He put Bill Presser on the labor ladder, and he taught Danny Greene the rungs.

At age twenty-six, Danny Greene was a power among the longshoremen. Very tough and fearless, both with his longshoremen and with the stevedore companies that furnished the work, Greene was Jimmy-Cagney-handsome and had a fabled charisma. The members elected him president. Even his chief opponent, Chauncey Baker, claims, "Danny could have been the greatest labor leader in this country. He saw the future. He had ideas."

"We Will Choose the Men"

At the beginning of his presidency, Greene presided over dockside chaos. Each stevedore company had its own hiring boss. When a stevedore company was hiring, longshoremen would assemble at that company's shape-up. The hiring boss might select fifty men to work the ship before putting up his hands, "That's all for today." The men would leave, except for a group of non-union favorites of the hiring boss. He would wave them in.

Those not selected would then rush over to another stevedore terminal, but often too late. The other terminal had hired "off the street."

Greene stopped that. "The union will hold the hiring hall in one central place. Tell us how many gangs you need. We will choose the men." He made that work.

The first such hiring hall was in the Marion Building, built by the descendants of Captain Bradley. Greene became tyrannically powerful on the docks. He flaunted the power, boasting that if crossed he would shut down the Port. And he could do it. His coercive hostility toward the stevedore companies was adopted by the rank and file. The employer was the enemy. Work stoppages and cargo shrinkages were winked at by Greene. His coterie of close friends in the union were wild, notably vice president Leon (Skip) Ponikvar, who carried weapons in his car and was accused of firing on a departing foreign vessel.

The Executive Offices

Under Weaver, "Union headquarters," Greene laughed, "was a closet with a packing crate desk and a light bulb on a cord." Greene changed that, too. His own spacious office had plush green carpet and rich mahogany furniture. The desk decoration was a stiletto stabbed into a block of cork. He furnished a board room with a huge mahogany table and specially designed and built cushioned chairs. He was stylish, especially in his own wardrobe.

The battle between Greene and the stevedore companies escalated. The stevedores wanted to be able to select certain men, or at least refuse men they considered troublemakers or cargo thieves.

Greene's moves embarrassed stevedore companies with their customers, drove some ships away, and hurt business. But Greene enjoyed personal power at any cost to the city.

A change was coming.

In another part of town Chauncey Baker, age eighteen, was working two jobs, one at Apex Manufacturing and the other with the railroad at $2.08 per hour. In 1956 the railroad laid him off for months; then the Apex job folded.

Danny Greene, recognizing a tough young kid, said, "Come down to the docks."

Baker was soon working so much on the docks that he had to quit the railroad. "Dock pay was only a dollar seventy-five an hour," he remembers, "but you could work a lot of hours."

After the Seaway opening there was work for every longshoreman. Danny Greene needed more men. Chauncey Baker brought him more. But these were different. They were Baker's young school classmates from Collinwood.

In 1959 Chauncey ran for business agent of the local. With the room packed with his boyhood friends from Collinwood, he won the job.

In this job he did the hiring, bringing in still more Collinwood youths.

Actually young Baker was somewhat in the mold of the classic dock boss, except he was not a talker. Not large, he was hard muscled and projected a short-fused, commanding personality. He understood the power of building a personal team.

Meanwhile Chauncey's brother, John, quit school at sixteen. He became a tear-sheet boy at the *Plain Dealer* in 1957. The job was to clip ads for advertisers to use in merchandising. He worked his way up to top tear-sheet boy, then into the dispatch department. However, in 1959 he asked Chauncey to help him get into the longshoremen's union. John Baker paid his $210 initiation fee.

Two years later Danny Greene appointed John secretary-treasurer. By then Chauncey was vice president *and* business agent.

The Baker brothers are very different. John is a large man and voluble. Chauncey is a reined-in explosion. Muscular, trim, and of medium height, Chauncey speaks little and quietly, but radiates a certain impatience. Ten swollen knuckles suggest a history about which few inquire.

In the 1960s and early 1970s, the longshoremen came into their best times. There were ships. If a man wanted, he could work eighty hours a week. During a New York dock strike that diverted cargoes to Lakes ports, 410 men in Local 1317 logged 436,000 man-hours. Chauncey Baker remembers, "At the time, Local 1317 was like a family—all from Collinwood."

"The Volunteers"

Even during these good times friction developed. Theoretically, to build a headquarters, Danny Greene had established a certain practice: on the days when grain ships came in, he asked volunteers to contribute their pay to a building fund. At first men volunteered willingly, though usually it was the same group of men. But later it became obvious that those who did not volunteer did not get called for other work.

"Chauncey, Maybe We Should Part"

After awhile, seeing no signs of a headquarters building plans, the volunteers became restive, then suspicious. Chauncey and John Baker, also volunteering on the grain ships, began receiving heated complaints. When these turned into a reluctance to work the grain ships free, Chauncey went to Greene. "Danny, we've got to stop the grain ship volunteering."

"No. We continue."

The July 4th holiday weekend was approaching. Greene said, "If you don't want to tell them, I'll do it." Greene then added, "Chauncey, maybe we should part. You go back on the docks."

Greene created three pier bosses and gave Chauncey Baker the smallest dock area, reducing Baker's exposure to the membership and his influence among the men. For Greene's comfort, Baker was too popular among the membership. He had recruited most of them from Collinwood. They were his friends.

Greene later called John Baker into his office, "Where do you stand in this argument, John?"

"Blood's thicker than water. I'm with my brother."

Within days, John Baker was out of the office and onto the docks.

Finally some member came out with a petition to get rid of Greene. The signatures were sent to ILA headquarters in New York. New York established a trusteeship for Local 1317.

By that time the *Plain Dealer* and the Labor Department were inquiring into the "volunteering" and what was happening to the money the volunteers turned over to the union.

To appoint a new president for the local, the trustee called three meetings, the critical one at the Pic-Carter Hotel, presided over by David Connor, ILA's international vice president. The meeting included the lawyer for Teamster president James Hoffa and two other Teamsters. The Teamsters wanted to control the docks. Chauncey Baker was present, "But they didn't want me for president. They said it would be just like putting Danny Greene back in."

In the course of the meeting, Chauncey Baker recalls the critical interchange. "Hoffa's lawyer said to me, 'you took orders from Babe Triscaro.'"

"No. I took no orders from Triscaro. I took my orders from Danny Greene. He was my boss."

At that point the Teamster lawyer's rebuttal profanely impugned the honesty of Mr. Baker, igniting his very low flash point. The attorney landed face-up on the hotel carpeting.

That's when Mr. Connor announced, "That's my man."

Baker, president of Local 1317, explains very quietly, "That's how I got my job."

Chauncey Baker went on to become district vice president and then international third vice president of ILA. John Baker, meanwhile, advanced to become Great Lakes District vice president, then Great Lakes District president and international vice president of ILA. Thus, the leadership in the Great Lakes District, once seated in Green Bay and once in Buffalo, had shifted to Cleveland. The Bakers are the only two brothers on an international board of any union in the United States.

Cleveland's Port has had no longshoreman strike in over three decades. Many alumni of Local 1317 who went on to big careers in business and law now brag about having been longshoremen in 1317. The *Plain Dealer* headlines began to change.

Scars of Violence Fade from City's Waterfront

A waterfront, any waterfront—in London, Calcutta, New York or Cleveland—carries a stigma of mystery, violence and corruption.

The stigma implies that only the quick and the mighty survive the rigors of the waterfront.

This stigma in many cases, is more fact than fiction.

For years the Cleveland waterfront had been racked by violence, theft and labor disputes and, prior to a year ago, by corrupt union leadership.

Today in Cleveland, for the time, at least, something has happened. The stigma deserves to be erased.

It was nearly a year ago The Plain Dealer exposed corruption in the leadership of Local 1317 of the International Longshoremen's Association, which resulted in a purge.

Since the start of the Great Lakes shipping season last spring, the crime rate has dropped, union-management relations have improved and production has increased. The atmosphere along the docks seems to exude cooperation among all who toil there.

Lt. Jack F. Delaney, head of the Police Department's Ports and Harbors Unit, spoke about the improved situation in his office at Burke Lakefront Airport recently.

"First of all," he said, "you have to give a lot of credit to Baker and the longshoremen's union."

Chauncey J. Baker, elected president of Local 1317 in May, replaced Daniel J. Greene, the waterfront boss who was indicted by a federal grand jury last year on charges of embezzling union funds. He is awaiting trial.

The indictment followed a series of articles by The Plain Dealer which revealed that Greene and an aide, Leon J. (Skip) Ponikvar, had stolen union funds.

"He (Baker) told his men in no uncertain terms that the union would not tolerate any stealing from the docks," Lt. Delaney said.

"There have been only 10 cases of thievery reported so far this year," the lieutenant said, crossing his fingers. "There were 37 last year."

Chauncey J. Baker is a man of few words. He does not elaborate upon the job he is doing nor the job the union is doing.

What does Baker think of the theft problem? He hands you a sheet of paper.

It was a memorandum and it said:

"Anyone who steals property from the premises of any employer, ship, dock or the union or who, without authority, has on his person or belongings any property being shipped through the Port of Cleveland shall be subject to penalties by the executive board. Criminal conviction for any offense relating to property of an employer or being shipped through the Port of Cleveland shall bar a man from employment through the union hiring hall."

"Ever catch anyone stealing?" Baker was asked.

"Just one, that's all, just one," he said. Baker did not elaborate.

He did say that production was up on the docks and the attitude of the men was better now that no one was forcing them.

Recently, the Cleveland Stevedore Co. hired three union members to act as foremen and Baker talked about this briefly.

"Everyone is saying you are doing a good job down here, Chauncey," the reporter said.

"Let our actions speak for themselves," Baker replied.

Christopher C. Morton, operations manager of Cleveland Stevedore, talked briefly about the atmosphere on the lakefront.

"This is the first time we have seen a concrete effort on the part of the union to cooperate," Morton said.

"Ever since our meeting in April things have been going along without any major problems."

Morton said production is up and he believes there is a keen interest on the part of the union to make Cleveland a better port. Production is measured by how swiftly a cargo can be unloaded.

Baker perks up when the talk gets around to production and it was obvious that he was proud of some of the accomplishments of his men.

"There was a captain in here last month who told me we have a better operation for unloading steel than they do in New York," Baker said.

"And you know that Jap boat we had out there two days ago? Well it was supposed to be ready to go at 3 in the afternoon and we got it out at 11 P.M. the day before."

There will be 550 to 600 ships with import goods from countries other than Canada arriving in Cleveland before the shipping season closes in December.

Baker said there are about 240 longshoremen who will make a living from unloading these ships.

A longshoreman who talked a few minutes with a reporter said things were 100% better than they had ever been in the five years he's been on the docks.

"No problems," said another.

"We do our job," a young man about 23 years old said.

No one elaborates.

Now it's quiet on the waterfront. According to Lt. Delaney, there has been only one beating reported this year. Theft is at mid-year low.

The five column headline in the *Plain Dealer,* November 14, 1966, read:

Greene Indicted on 7 Counts
Ex-Dock Czar's Top Aide Also to
Face Trial

Daniel J. Greene, 34, dethroned waterfront union czar, yesterday was accused by a federal grand jury of embezzling union funds and trying to cover up by falsifying Landrum-Griffin Act reports.

Indicted with Greene, former president of International Longshoremen's Association Local 1317, was his burly aide, Leon J. (Skip) Ponikvar, 25.

The grand jury indicted Greene on five counts of embezzling union funds and two counts of filing false union records with the government.

Maximum penalties on all counts against Greene, if convicted, total 27 years in jail and $70,000 in fines.

Ponikvar was indicted with Greene for conspiracy to embezzle union funds. He was also charged with making out a payroll that contained fictitious names and falsifying the amounts of wages due union members.

Greene was convicted by a federal jury on five counts of embezzling union funds and falsifying records to the government.

The appeals court in Cincinnati overturned the conviction.

However, in Greene's new line of work, firechasing, he got in with some very bad company. In 1968, he pulled into his dentist's crowded parking lot in Lyndhurst. Suddenly a parking space opened up directly in front of him and he pulled right in. When his dental work was finished, he returned to the parking lot, got into his car, and turned on the ignition. Suddenly the car right next to him blew up, killing Daniel Greene.

At this writing Cleveland's longshoremen are highly regarded by stevedore companies and foreign captains.

16

The Pilot

"Steer two two five."

"Two two five, sir."

"Half ahead."

"Half ahead."

"Seaway Welland control. *Atlantic Hawk* out of Buffalo calling. This is the pilot. Destination Toledo. ETA: Oh four three oh. Course two two five."

"Full ahead now."

"Full ahead."

It was not the captain giving the orders; it was the pilot, Don Johns.

"Toledo tug office. Toledo tug office. *Atlantic Hawk* calling."

"Tug office. Go to channel ten."

"*Atlantic Hawk*. Pilot speaking. Did the agent arrange two tugs for me? What time? Over."

"Tug office to *Atlantic Hawk*. Oh seven fifteen at Anderson's Lay Up Dock. Tugs *Virginia* and the *Tennessee*. Over."

"Then what time do we move up to the elevator? Over."

"About ten hundred hours. Over."

"Too soon. The master needs seven to ten hours to deballast. I'll call you just before I enter the channel."

Two hours before this, Captain Geraci, master of the *Atlantic Hawk* out of Greece, looked up at the six-foot-four-inch Don Johns who ducked through the doorway into the pilothouse. Johns wore a business suit and necktie. George Scuggin, administrator of pilotage, coached all pilots, "You'll be the first American some of these foreign crews will see. Look the part."

They shook hands and the captain turned his ship over to Don Johns, veteran pilot, first-class license 577116, any tonnage. Johns had brought about 1,200 ships safely to port. No accidents.

Ships entering the Seaway require a pilot, or rather several, one for each district as the ship moves up the Seaway. Johns would pilot the *Hawk* upstream to Port Colborne with stops at Cleveland and Toledo.

A sea captain is a monarch. How does he feel about putting his ship in the hands of a pilot? Saltwater captains are not timid men. But, accustomed to wide oceans with miles of water on all quarters, Captain Geraci, like most saltwater masters, was shaken on his first Seaway trip to find his ship walled in, port and starboard, by high rock escarpments in the St. Lawrence. Then, when the *Hawk* entered the locks at the Welland with walls of cement inches from his gunwales, Captain Geraci perspired.

The pilot knows the channels, the traffic, shoals, rocks, islands, effects of weather in different stretches of the Seaway. He knows how to come through six bridges to get out of Toledo in the dark, staying in the narrow fourteen-mile-long channel to get to open water. The pilots know the complex Chicago port and the St. Marys River and the upbound and downbound approaches to the Soo, and they know the Whitefish Bay graveyard.

Good, experienced pilotage is important to the ports. A slightly bad landing can knock apart a dock for a six-figure repair.

When Johns came aboard, he asked the pilot he relieved for any special information; for example, he learned that sixty revolutions make seven knots. Then he checked out the pilothouse. He always inspects the wheel. Is the gyro correct? Is the radar in working order? He checks the chadburn and rudder and engine RPM indicators. He gets some more information from the captain or the watch officer—about equipment, draft, how many revolutions for minimum speed.

The Making of a Pilot

A pilot is usually a man of enormous experience. Don Johns has worked waters all over the world, except Spain.

As a young man he began shipping out of Mobile for South America and other continents.

As Hitler began invading Europe, Don came to Cleveland to court a young woman he had known previously in the South. Three days after Pearl Harbor, he married her.

Working on the ore boats, he wanted to get a pilot's license. He had sufficient sea time for a license but needed to go to the Maritime Academy for the book learning and exams. The class was full. Before the next class was called, he was drafted. His draft board in Baltimore said go back on the Lakes where you're needed or go into the army. Don went back on the Lakes.

He shipped out in 1941 as wheelsman on the *William Nottingham,* a small ore carrier with just eleven hatches, on the Cleveland-Duluth run. She was owned by the Great Lakes Steamship Company.

The following year he sailed for Hanna. He received his papers as first-class pilot—Buffalo, Gary, Duluth—and was promoted to third mate.

Temporarily he went with the great Pittsburgh Steamship Company. Then, for twenty-one years, he sailed Shenango Furnace boats as second mate, first mate, and relief captain.

When Shenango was sold he went with the tankers as first mate and relief captain. He did not like tankers. In 1970 he went with the Bethlehem Steel Fleet as third mate. The way the shipping recession was going, he felt he would be out of a job, so he applied for pilotage.

In 1971 the Great Lakes Pilotage Association called. They had an opening, but he had to have a master's license. He had the sea time, but he had to go through the written exams.

First Job

His first pilotage assignment was to take a grain boat out of Toledo to Port Colborne. He was relieved because she was scheduled to leave in daylight; he did not wish to start a pilotage career feeling his way out through Toledo's six bridges at night. But the vessel ended up sailing at midnight.

Getting the Call

The Canadian pilotage office is at Port Colborne. The U.S. pilotage office, housing the radio dispatchers, is at Port Huron. In the office a large board lists the pilots in rotation, showing those at rest and those available for duty. A pilot gets twelve hours' rest before being put on the bottom of the "ready" list.

When Don Johns's turn comes up, he gets a phone call telling him which ship and where to meet her. He has two hours to pack and make travel arrangements. If the ship is far from his home base, he may fly to it; if within three hours drive time, he will drive the pilotage car and leave it at the port.

Before he comes aboard, the pilot will have obtained considerable information about the ship. At some ports the pilot can walk aboard, right off the dock. But if the ship is underway, he boards by rope ladder from the pilot boat. Climbing a swinging rope ladder to the pilot house in weather is a high-stress move.

Indeed, stress goes with the job. Every time a marine pilot whispers a large ship up to a dock, his heart rate rises to about the same level as a driver who has just avoided an accident. If he must board the ship while it is in motion, the heart rate rises even higher. Day-to-day risk and uncertainty are the pilot's companions. He does not know when he will be called next, how large the ship will be, with whom he'll be working, where he will be going, or what the weather will be.

The pilot does not touch any control, except possibly the radar. He controls by verbal orders, which are repeated by the watch officer. Johns has certain rules he follows. "When [the pilot] give[s] an order, for example 'Dead ahead slow,' [he] want[s] to make sure the watch officer repeats it exactly. That might sound simple, but even though a foreign officer speaks English, he may have a certain accent which leaves you in doubt, or sounds like a different command." Also, since not all of Captain Geraci's crew speak English, the captain sometimes translates Don's commands into Greek. There is also a danger in sound-alike words. *Sta'b'd* in English means "right"; in Russian it sounds like a word for "left."

Johns has another rule for bringing a ship safely to port while receiving radio navigation information from tugs agents, stevedores, Coast Guard—"If you don't see it, don't believe it."

Johns always used two tugs going into Toledo. "That channel is only a hundred feet wide and you never know for sure when one of those bridges is not going to open."

He listens to the radio traffic. He may hear, "This is the tug *Texas* downbound with the ship *Mather*. I'm at the north end." The pilot may elect to slow down or speed up so that the two ships and three tugs will meet where there is the most room. The captains generally deal with their own agents by radio. But if a captain is having some difficulty with the idiomatic English of one of his agent's staff, the pilot may oblige, as in the case of the *Atlantic Hawk.*

"This is Don Johns calling for Captain Geraci, *Atlantic Hawk*. The captain requests, would you arrange U.S. currency for the crew to take ashore. Over."

"To *Atlantic Hawk. Atlantic Hawk.* No problem. How much? Over."

A layman watching a ship docking sees nothing happening. But in a sense it is the busiest time of the trip. The vessel seems to be practically motionless. That's because everyone involved in landing this monster knows the enormous destructive momentum of a hundred thousand tons barely moving. It can tear out bridges and docks and stove in hull plates.

Therefore, approaching Toledo, Johns calls the stevedore company. "Need four linesmen at TOT Berth One." As he approaches the berth, Pilot Johns calls to his tugs.

"Hello, *Pennsylvania.*"

"*Pennsylvania.*"

"Please let me know my draft astern."

"Nineteen."

"*Tennessee,* what do I have forward?"

"Twenty-six."

"Thank you. Gentlemen, we're going in head up."

"Repeat please."

"We're going in head up."

As he brings the *Hawk* parallel to the dock, but off fifty feet, Johns begins talking to the tugs and to his bow and stern and 'midship lookouts and to the watch officer.

"Slow astern."

"Slow astern."

"Stop."

"Stop."

"She's coming in here nice. Looks like we'll be forty feet off."

You can hardly see her move, but to the pilot 100,000 tons is racing toward the dock. "Bow watch. How much now?"

"Twenty-four feet."

"Stern watch. How much?"

"About twenty."

"*Tennessee.* Give us a nudge, gentle."

The *Hawk* is moved broadside toward the dock.

"OK. *Virginia*...now." After seconds, "*Virginia,* too much. Cut her back."

The pilot asks, "Bow watch, how is it?"

"About fifteen feet, sir."

"Stern watch?"

"About fifteen."

"Bow watch?"

"About eight."

"Stern?"

"Still fifteen."

"*Virginia,* will you come alongside a quarter."

After a little while, "*Virginia,* I'm alongside."

"Give me a little nudge. But wait till they get those lines out of water. I'll tell you when."

After a minute, "*Virginia.* Now."

The *Hawk* was snugged up to the bollards. Captain Geraci asked, "You going ashore for awhile, Mr. Johns?"

"Not till I see them get the strain line on her, Captain."

Day and night, in all weather, pilots direct ships along the Seaway narrows and safely to port. The responsibility is heavy. The safety of a crew and a vessel, which with cargo may weigh in at a hundred million dollars, depends on a pilot's directions.

17

The Engineer

Young Sook Reid, chief engineer, Army Corps of Engineers, with shoulder-length black hair under a white hard hat, yelled over the deck noise on the dredge *Rhode Island* to white-haired Jack Keough. "Need your paperwork in by Friday, Jack." Three decades earlier Keough lost a bid for the world middleweight championship to Randy Turpin in England, but lately he's won dredging contract bids for the Port.

Later that day on the windy breakwall, Reid put two rocks on an engineering drawing and addressed three scuba divers. "Before we sign off on this repair, I want you to look especially close at this juncture of the old wall and the repair."

Reid was instructing the divers on inspecting the 3,300-foot repair of the wall damaged by storms. For the Corps of Engineers, Reid was in charge of the coastline from Sandusky to the Pennsylvania line for harbor improvements and maintenance and flood and erosion control. Reid explained, "Where the repair joins the old wall, see if the reinforcing piling overlaps like this." The divers studied the drawing.

Sook Reid, only twenty-nine at that time, was in charge of millions of dollars of contracts for dredging and harbor repairs and other shoreline maintenance along the division's coastline.

This is not a once-in-a-while action. Even shoreline residents do not see that ports do not automatically remain ports. They must be constantly renewed. They fill with silt brought down by the rivers. Every spring the Corps takes soundings to see if a twenty-seven-foot channel for shipping sustains. The shores erode, breakwalls crumble, docks get rammed, bootleg effluent flows in via new illegal pipes. New land wants to be created to add to the shore. This work goes on steadily except during the ice season. The Corps of Engineers uses private contractors for the work. That breakwall repair contract Reid was supervising was for $5,470,000. Great Lakes Dredge & Dock had a contract that year to dredge 355,000 cubic yards of silt and barge it to Gordon Park to create an eighty-acre park extension that cost $2,597,800 for the part of the work done that year.

Engineers have always recreated this Cleveland Port. Samuel Orth, historian and president of the Cleveland School Board in 1905, published a history in 1910 that gives a remarkable picture of this engineer-built port. He described how, after an angry meeting of citizens in 1825, A. W. Walworth, warehouse owner, traveled to Washington and demanded a meeting with the congresssional committee on rivers and harbors. He told them something needed to be done to prevent the Cuyahoga from annually forming a sandbar, obstructing navigation. He argued passionately. The Congress appropriated $5,000 for building a pier at the mouth of the Cuyahoga. The first

winter wrecked the pier. Orth's account explains the next steps:

Captain Q. W. Maruice of the Corps of Engineers submitted a plan for closing the mouth of the old river bed, thereby compelling the river to flow straight into the lake, and then building two jetties about two hundred feet apart into the lake to the depth of twelve feet of water. It was estimated that this would cost $27,653.91. In March, 1827 Congress appropriated $10,000 for carrying out the project. A dam two hundred and fifty-five feet long was thrown across the bed of the river to deflect the current and in the spring of 1828 the river . . . made a straight cut through the bar to the lake.

In 1831 the west pier was completed and a beacon light erected on its outer end. By 1833 a channel eleven feet deep had been secured. The piers were built of timber frames resting on the lake bottom and filled with stone. The construction was evidently not calculated to withstand the onslaught of heavy seas, for they were constantly in need of repairs.

In September, 1864, Colonel T. J. Cram of the Corps of Engineers reported that the west pier was falling to pieces and that the east pier was pre-empted by railroad companies who were using it for wharves, while at the entrance of the channel a sand bar had formed preventing vessels of a greater draught than eleven feet from entering. He recommended . . . that Congress should pass an act prohibiting the use of government piers by private parties . . . but it was many years before the railroads were dispossessed of the east pier.

To the year 1875, less than a million government dollars had been spent on the Cleveland harbor improvements. In that year a board of Army engineers convened in Cleveland to investigate the full needs of the harbor. It recommended and implemented several improvements, and Samuel Orth reported in 1883 that the following situation existed: ". . . leaving an opening into the new harbor of about thirty feet. The west breakwater was completed in 1883, a total length of 7,130 feet, forming a harbor of refuge with an area of a hundred acres for anchorage in depths varying from seventeen to twenty-nine feet."

The board also recommended that a harbormaster be appointed and that a strong seagoing tug be purchased to be used in placing vessels that could not be handled by the river tugs.

The commerce of Cleveland was growing so constantly and the art of shipbuilding so rapidly, that before the proposed plan could be entirely carried out, the marine interests of Cleveland vigorously urged enlargement and modification. The War Department ordered a second board of engineers to meet in Cleveland on September 10, 1884, to study the situation. This board recommended an eastern breakwater.

Lieutenant Colonel Jared Smith took charge of the work. He discovered that the old piers were in ruins.

The first large wharves built on the lakefront east of the river were begun in 1894, two docks with a large slip between them. These were equipped with coal-loading machines with a capacity of twenty cars per hour.

The Development of the Inner Harbor

When the first surveying party landed at the mouth of the Cuyahoga, it found that a substantial sandbar closed the river's entrance to large boats. The spring floods usually washed the bar away so that boats could pass up the river to the foot of Superior Street, but late-summer storms built new sandbars. Boats were forced to anchor outside the mouth and unload by lighters. As the harbor was unprotected, these vessels were often damaged by storms while at anchor.

In 1828 the harbor admitted vessels of seven-and-a-half-feet draught. The townspeople were delighted. The *Herald* recorded that "schooners and steamboats daily come up to our wharves and load and discharge their cargoes." By March 1829, however, the water had fallen again to five feet at the mouth of the river, and there was a sandbar awaiting the spring freshets. The building of the cribs was delayed because of what Orth called quicksand.

In 1837 the town surveyed the outer harbor, planning a breakwater. This was the first agitation for building a mole or outer harbor.

Cleveland repeatedly petitioned the federal government for harbor development money, acting as if it was owed to them. By 1850 the citizens had come to believe that they could not depend on Congress for the development of their harbor.

In 1854 the inner harbor was so narrow that boats lying at wharves on either side seriously obstructed the passageway. By 1855 the congestion had become so acute that much trade, especially in grain, was lost to the harbor. The perennial sandbar persisted at the entrance.

Finally the city learned that, if the inner harbor was to be developed, it would be done with local money.

In 1870 the mayor complained, "the dredging of the river is a source of continued expense" and the engineer "reports that every freshet makes a sand bar." Half of the expense of dredging was shared by the property owners fronting the river, the other half by the city. They attempted to have the depth of channel keep pace with the increasing draught of the vessels. In 1874 the depth was fourteen feet. But in his annual address, Mayor Payne said, "But if vessels drawing twelve or fourteen feet of water stick on sand bars in the mouth of the harbor or lodge in the mud before they reach their destined docks, as was true last season, the best lake trade will shun us."

Thus a succession of engineers are part of a long history of building the Port. Young Sook Reid continues the work. Those Corps of Engineer captains and majors and colonels would respect Reid and would be surprised.

Reid emigrated from South Korea in 1972, became a U.S. citizen in 1977, and received a B.S. degree in civil engineering from Cleveland State in 1980. Beginning a co-op program with the Army Corps of Engineers, Reid worked hard to become chief engineer of the Sandusky to Pennsylvania district in 1984.

That is unusual enough; but it becomes more so when one meets Ms. Reid in person and learns that her four sisters are also graduate engineers.

18

The Care and Handling

A decade and a half of successful operations should earn the Port fair weather and calm water. The management consistently raised the asset value, earned income to maintain the property, pay the bills and attract business. They accomplished this in a thin market in the face of rail competition and a near shut-out from the container business. The Port extended that record to two good business years in 1985 and 1986.

Yet those two years of good performance would be so rocked by political, financial, and navigational storms as to threaten the very existence of the Authority . . . again.

The first blow weakened the crew.

Anthony J. Russo, special consultant to the Board since 1983, had secured grants for the Port in the amounts of $32,000 and $13,000. On January 11, 1985, the Board voted to renew his contract for another year. As director of government relations for the Port, Russo had been knowledgeable and shrewd. Tom Burke recalled, "Tony knew how politics intertwines with business, he knew who to call (and who not to), and his advice was always solid."

Unfortunately, Tony Russo died in March 1985.

This was the first of a series of blows to the ranks. In spring there had been a lot of publicity concerning Board secretary Arnold Pinkney and his indictment, trial, and eventual conviction on a felony charge. The Board accepted Pinkney's resignation. John J. Dwyer was elected the new secretary, but Pinkney's seat on the Board was not immediately filled. A new post was created, director of administration, filled by Hugh Tobin.

In the first month of 1986, the maritime community was stunned to learn that Frank A. Palladino, Jr., of the Ohio Bulk Transfer Company had been killed in an air crash.

Just a few days later, two Board members resigned, Campbell Elliott and John Dwyer. The latter's resignation left the Board with only one director with maritime background, the chairman.

These withdrawals, plus Joseph Berger's term ending, left the Board struggling to achieve quorum with only six active members. In 1986, the three officers were elected by a total of four votes: Jay Ehle, chairman; Carmen Parise, vice chairman; and Sterling Glover, secretary.

Mayor George Voinovich soon appointed two directors: local real estate developer and former banker, Carl D. Glickman, would replace Berger; and former City of Cleveland law director, Thomas E. Wagner, replaced Elliott. Theirs would be a baptism by fire.

In the friends-as-opponents game, even after sixteen years, the city still played its annual delay of approval of the lease. However, everyone knew the new annual rent would be $500,000.

Special events parking had a contentious history. Ameripark took over the special events parking contract for an agreed $40,000 lump sum. In April this was changed to interval payments to total $20,000 by the beginning of football season.

However, when proposed plans for the inner harbor were announced, the Port learned the project would absorb about 1,900 parking spaces east of the stadium. The Stadium Corporation asked the city for replacement parking, and the city asked the Port to provide the space west of the stadium. Ehle estimated this would consume about a fourth of Port property. One suggestion was to demolish Warehouse A for parking. Another had the Stadium Corporation razing the Parcel Post Building, using relocation funds from the budget of the inner harbor project. This discussion prompted other questions: Will the inner harbor really be built? Will the Browns remain in Cleveland? Will a domed stadium be built? The chairman stated that in any case the Port and its business must be protected.

The search for suitable tenants for the Parcel Post Building seemed futile; the Board sought viable alternatives. The building needed massive repairs for any tenant, but tearing it down could cost as much as $750,000. Burke suggested the area would bring in a substantial income if the building were demolished. The footers could be preserved for possible future use. The question of

Parcel Post Building use continued throughout 1985 without resolution.

The West 9th Street Corporation leased the building but in the spring of 1986 was in default on payments. The Port filed a lawsuit. Serving notice to the principals, Joseph Loconti and Joseph Singerman, was a problem, however, as their addresses changed.

Despite this and other problems, some on the Board felt there was still a chance to save the Parcel Post Building, but most felt a cut-off date on receiving new proposals was warranted. Finally, a joint meeting of five Board committees on March 25, 1986, recommended demolition. The foundation would be preserved, and the Corps of Engineers approved use of suitable material from the demolition as fill on the lakefront at Dock 22.

Demolition of the Parcel Post Building decreased the Port's equity by $198,802.40. The work fell so far behind schedule that it angered the directors.

Protecting the Turf

Waterfront property in Cleveland became precious.

In Greater Cleveland a crowd of individuals, organizations, and governments had designs on the Port's waterfront for developments that do not need water. But ships can *only* work on water.

In February 1986, the Port still had no long-term lease on the land with the City of Cleveland. It appeared obvious that the city had pigeon-holed this lease. In May a formal Board committee renewed negotiations with the city. The committee was comprised of Parise, Glickman, Glover, Wagner, and, of course, Ehle, serving ex-officio on every committee.

This long-awaited agreement between the city and the Port committee was reached but needed full Board approval. Presented to them in November 1980, the agreement provided a forty-year lease starting at $500,000 per year. The agreement on three of the docks could be terminated after five years with specified advance notice, with provisions for rent reduction. The city required the Port to provide 1,200 vehicle parking spaces for sports events at the stadium. The agreement gave the Port the right to purchase Docks 24 and 26 at any time. The city agreed to vacate West 9th Street north of the railroad and exchange certain parcels.

With few changes, the Board approved; but the lease still needed City Council approval.

The North Cost Development Corporation made Chairman Ehle a member of its executive committee and the official negotiator between that corporation and the Corps of Engineers in relation to the development of the Cleveland harbor.

This was a step forward in the rocky city-Port relationship—the Port trying to defend its position and property while the city waffled in its thinking about whether to sell, keep, or lease property that it might want for other uses. Now Port and city would be in a working relationship on lakefront development plans.

The chairman accepted even more responsibility when he was elected to the executive committee of the Cleveland Growth Association to act as liaison with the Corps of Engineers. This strengthened the Port's ability to hold its waterfront.

Back to the Main Mission

The business of the Port is shipping.

Amid all the other inland oriented involvements, the management kept its eyes seaward. The business of the Port is attracting the ships, unloading the ships, loading the ships, helping the shippers.

To sustain efficiency of Port operations, in 1985 the Authority computerized information systems.

For attracting ships to Cleveland, the Authority funded a trade mission by its marketing director, James J. Cobbett, to Spain, Italy, Portugal, and Yugoslavia. The mission was sponsored by the St. Lawrence Sea-

way Development Corporation. Tom Burke attended the Ports, Transport & Equipment 1986 trade fair in Rotterdam. Cleveland was the only Great Lakes port in attendance. Burke also made sales trips to Antwerp, Hamburg, London, and Paris.

In the spring of 1985, the Authority approved the Cleveland Stevedore Company, Federal Marine Terminals, Inc., and Ohio Bulk Transfer Company as terminal operators. The Port also considered Coakley Terminals, Inc., but tabled the decision based on rumors of Coakley's financial difficulties. This also prompted examination of requirements for approving terminal operators.

The actual activity on the docks was generally good despite some weak spots and some major navigation disasters.

Shipment of ore from Dock 20 had all but stopped, as had overseas shipments of PL480 food cargoes. Although container shipments at the Port in July were up, container business was generally weak. The Port's efforts to continue in the container business contributed to the small, but steady, stream of these shipments. In April 1985 one shipment by SCM Corporation brought sixty containers of rutile sand (titanium dioxide) from Rio de Janeiro, bringing the total for the month to eighty-three—well ahead of the previous April.

Also in April, Foreign Free Trade Subzones were approved for General

Motors Corporation in Lordstown; the Ford Motor Company in Lorain; and the Park Corporation at the Cleveland Tank Plant in Cleveland.

There was also ongoing Board exploration of Foreign Free Trade Zones, Warehouse A, and the assigning of berths to the Cleveland Stevedore Company, issues that were approved in a special meeting on May 28.

The MV *Diana,* a Netumar Line vessel, called at the Port of Cleveland with a very large movement of presses from Brazil for the Chrysler Corporation in Twinsburg, Ohio. The shipment included several containers and two very heavy and extra-wide machines.

The navy frigate USS *Stark* lured some forty thousand visitors to the docks.

During one of the busiest times of the 1985 season, on October 14, a wall in Lock 7 collapsed, closing the Welland Canal for twenty-four days. Before the lock could reopen, it had to be drained so that Canadian workers could clear the debris, erect steel braces, and pour tons of concrete. Ten ships in the first fifty stranded by the collapse had been bound for Cleveland. As the first one, the Polish *Ziemia Suwalska,* started through the Welland on November 6, longshoremen in Cleveland ended their forced lay-up and headed for the docks.

Shipping resumed with great urgency as captains went full ahead to beat the ice that could force costly winter lay-up in the Lakes. But efforts to finish the season smoothly were stymied again on December 1, when a freighter rammed another bridge near Quebec and caused more delays.

Additionally, on December 4, twenty ships were backed up waiting to get through the frozen locks at Sault St. Marie. In Cleveland, as many as five ships were unloading at one time in early December, still trying to beat the winter freeze. Perhaps it was this overflow of activity that allowed a Polish sailor to stroll off his ship unnoticed despite carrying a suitcase full of clothes. Newspapers were filled with stories of the sailor enjoying Cleveland's Polish community while waiting for word of political asylum from the federal government.

Import of steel was a double-edged sword for the ports. More imports meant more business, but it also meant less export of locally produced steel. Chairman Ehle summed up the feelings of the Board: "Imported steel is a fact of life. As long as steel is going to come into this country, we want it to come in through the Port of Cleveland."

General cargoes—ranging from the huge automotive stamping presses for General Motors and Chrysler to wines from Europe—were up 9 percent. The Buckeye Booster was used efficiently three times this season. The Port earned universal recognition as the number-one heavy-lift port on the Great Lakes.

Overall tonnage for 1985 showed a 19-percent increase, with the strongest growth (24 percent) registered by steel imports.

The first ship in 1986, MV *Project Europa*, arrived on April 8 with some of the General Motors cargo that would move through the Port over the next two years.

Ohio Bulk renewed its use of Dock 20 for the year. They guaranteed a minimum of $125,000; the lease, however, would be renegotiated. The lease with the Stadium Corporation was also renewed at $80,000 a year plus $1,500 per event after January 1, 1987. There was a 60-percent participation in the parking revenue if the parking exceeded 80,000 vehicles.

There was a slight increase in the number of international vessels calling at the Port in 1986. If the Canadians could be persuaded to forgo the 15-percent raise in Seaway tolls they were requesting, future prospects for the Great Lakes might continue to improve.

In mid-April two new Board members signed on. Patrick S. Parker was chairman of Parker Hannifin; and Fred M. Crosby, owner of a local retail furniture and appliance business, had a resumé studded with local, state, and national appointments from mayors, governors, and presidents, both Democrats and Republicans.

In mid-1985 the Board voted 5 to 1 not to renew the contract of the executive director. In addition to comments from friends and politicians on Burke's departure, there was response from the head of the Seaway, the mayor, and local business leaders regarding Burke's extravagant behavior. But Burke's professional and personable demeanor soon landed him a new position, as port director at Port Everglades in Fort Lauderdale, Florida, at a substantial salary increase.

The Port participated in a cluster of August events: the World Trade Development Club of the Columbus Area Chamber of Commerce conference; the U.S. Coast Guard Buoy Tender Conference in Cleveland; and the Harbor Expo '86 held in conjunction with promoting the Inner Harbor Project. A boardwalk carried people from the parking lot on the east side of the Cleveland Municipal Stadium across Erieside Avenue.

Throughout August, members of the Board interviewed sixteen applicants for executive director. In September, retired Rear Admiral Anthony Fugaro accepted the position at a salary of $58,000, plus a car.

Fugaro, a graduate of the U.S. Coast Guard Academy at New London, Connecticut, had served in San Juan, London, Germany, Copenhagen, and Antwerp before receiving his master's degree from George

Washington University in 1976. After thirty-two years with the Coast Guard, he retired in 1981 (from a post in Cleveland) and joined Great Lakes Towing as a vice president.

In December, the Board authorized Fugaro to participate in the Seaway sponsored European Trade Mission to be held in late February 1987. They hired John L. Townley as manager of Port operations.

Overall, tonnage declined about 8 percent in 1986, caused in part by a 15-percent decline in imported steel as a result of the federal government's reinstatement of foreign steel import quotas.

For the first time in years, the Port *exported* American-made steel. Tonnage was not significant, but it demonstrated that steel made in America was still competitive on the world market.

General cargo for the year was up 193 percent, due in large part to the many heavy-lift cargoes of computerized stamping presses brought in for upgrades at the Ohio plants of Chrysler and General Motors.

The Hidden Heart
and a Dog Named Cleveland

When the Polish vessel tied up late at night, she had aboard an ancient and beloved and very sick ship's dog. The ship's agent immediately went to work on the phone to find a veterinarian to attend the dog. Since no local veterinarian would make such a late house call, the agent worked his way out to neighboring towns. When his calls to forty miles away, east and west, brought no response, he reported to the Polish seaman. He would continue trying.

One English-speaking Polish seaman, fearing the delay would be fatal, found his way to the Seamen's Service and told the on-duty volunteer the problem. The volunteer phoned the Animal Protective League. Yes, they had a veterinarian on duty. He came to the ship. Unfortunately, he found the mascot's life fading too fast for treatment. He explained this to the circle of twelve Polish seamen surrounding him. The English-speaking seaman explained to them that all the doctor could do was put the dog to sleep. They nodded.

The veterinarian walked back to the Seamen's Service. He didn't look good. He explained what he had had to do.

"But you must have had to do that often."

"Not with twelve grown men standing around with tears running down their faces."

An hour later he was back at the ship, carrying a large and lively dog from the APL kennel. "I know it won't be the same, but. . ."

When the ship's cargo was discharged and the lines were about to be cast off, the English-speaking Polish seaman came running into the Seamen's Service with a handful of Polish money for the Animal Protective League and to announce they had named the dog—"He is Cleveland!"

Before the Seaway, but after the enlarging of some St. Lawrence River channels, many flags sailed into Great Lakes ports, the crews speaking many languages. The big ocean ports had welcomed the languages for years and visiting foreign crews felt some connection. However, Great Lakes ports in the early 1960s were not that cosmopolitan.

Mrs. Claire Howard was a Cleveland newspaper feature writer. Covering the city, she noted that visiting crews hung close to the dockside taverns, having no liaison to the sports events, museums, theaters, or anything much beyond the then-dim taverns in the Flats. She decided that Cleveland should greet these visitors better and help them more. She planted that thought with some high-level civic lions in town. Sometimes she planted the idea gently, other times briskly, laying on a touch of guilt.

Thus was born the Seamen's Service.

The support for the Service was quick and substantial. Furniture, carpets, lamps, offer of free printing came in to that first center located in the old Cleveland & Buffalo Transit Company's 9th Street Pier terminal. When that was torn down in 1969, the city donated space at Burke Lakefront Airport. However, when the foreign crews had trouble finding it, the Service moved in 1970 to the former office of Georgian Bay Line on the East 9th Street Pier.

By 1986, the Service had earned the recognition of several civic organizations. It was an important operation; it needed a good, permanent facility. The prime movers in making that happen included civic leaders and several organizations and private companies.

The new building was a strong advance; however, the great strength of the Service, which assists foreign seamen in hundreds of ways, is the corps of dedicated volunteers who do this work quietly, rain or shine, day or night and weekends. Among the volunteers is enough language capability that they can always find a volunteer who can communicate with any crew member.

What the existence of the Service says is "Welcome to Cleveland!"

19

Crosswinds, 1987–1989

"One If By Land . . ."

The threat was not from the sea. The next three years brought severe challenges to the Port Authority's very existence mixed with victorious celebrations. The Authority's own friends and sponsors threatened to destroy it, even while looking to it for great community benefits.

The general public, which would vote to renew the operating levy, was almost totally unaware of the Port. Except for stadium crowds, few even saw the ships; commuters along the shore at 60 m.p.h. only caught fleeting glimpses of the ships. Therefore, the Authority engaged the public relations firm Burges & Burges to bring the Port to the public.

Mayor George Voinovich promised his support for the Port's renewal levy, and he said he would do all he could to push the lease agreement through City Council. Although the *mayor* had signed the lease, it was not scheduled for review by City Council's city planning committee until May 13.

While waiting for this, the Authority learned that its friend and tenant, the Cleveland Stevedore Company, was making overtures to the city to take over the Port facilities.

While Board officers remained the same (Ehle, chairman; Parise, vice chairman; Glover, secretary), directors Deubel and George were replaced by Howard W. Broadbent and Michael G. Schneider. There had been a very important change in Board method—a shift to more intensive committee work. Through careful committee appointments by the chairman, many problems formerly wasting much exploratative debate in general Board meetings were now researched in committee, producing informed recommendations.

Mayor Voinovich urged the directors to involve the Port in Cleveland Civic Vision 2000, because "the Port of Cleveland is the backbone of the community." He suggested issuing bonds to develop Port property in anticipation of the loss of Dock 32 to the city.

Getting involved in the community while still preserving the Port average for ships was not often compatible. For example, in February the Great Lakes Historical Society accepted the ore carrier *William G. Mather* from the Cleveland Cliffs Corporation, hoping to use this historic ship as a living museum and locate it on North Coast Harbor. But the Port Authority was not in a position to offer any dock space for at least five years. The earnest volunteers who laboriously and lovingly restored the vessel found themselves confronted by several government bureaus with various regulations.

The Strategic Plan

Regarding the mayor's suggestion to get involved in Vision 2000, the Board had already designed the Port's strategic future development plan. It provided for marketing and promotion, facilities development, and more deliberate attention to the Port's relationship to the community and the outside world. It presented three main priorities: increasing employment and economic development; enhancing Port facilities; and strengthening public affairs. Initially Vision 2000 planned a parking garage and terminal warehouse adjacent to the Flats and the Cuyahoga River, which would benefit the Port with warehouse and dock space it would lose when the city reclaimed its docks and with easy-access parking to a revitalized and still-developing Flats. And the projects would have an economic impact on the community by creating construction jobs during start-up and permanent jobs when facilities became operational.

While the Board thanked Voinovich for his enthusiasm and advice, it emphatically explained that any planning for the future hinged on a signed lease with the city, and that lease was blocked in City Council.

The levy committee was very strong: Virgil Brown; Mary Rose Oakar; Bill McCarthy, president of Local 555 Natural Gas Workers Union for seventeen years; and Bill Williams of Huntington Bank. This levy, guaranteeing financing for the next five years, appeared on the November 1987 ballot and passed with 61 percent of the vote. It received voter approval in every ward in the city and every suburb in the county except two (where it lost by a total of nine votes).

Oakar, with the help of Congressman Louis Stokes, also pushed through an $11-million budget appropriation for Lake and harbor improvements, including dredging the inner harbor and formulating plans for a new berth for the Port.

But the Lease?

Despite the levy passage, November brought more friction with the city. The Port directors heard that City Council president George Forbes was entertaining proposals for other uses of Port facilities. The November 9, 1987, *Plain Dealer* editorialized: "The lease has languished since spring in council's Finance Committee whose chairman, Council President George L. Forbes, will neither release it nor explain his reticence. Other council members speculate that Forbes is sitting on the lease until plans for development around the North Coast Harbor project coalesce. Whenever that may be."

The staff was strengthened when the Port took advantage of Steve Pfeiffer's resignation from Cleveland Stevedores by hiring him as deputy director. Within two years, through his effort with the Ohio Department of Transportation, the Port was able to receive state grants for the first time. These enabled major renovation of Warehouse A in 1989, including new railroad tracks which permitted railcars to continuously load and unload inside the building, a heating/ventilation system to prevent corrosion and condensation on stored materials, and two new overhead cranes capable of lifting thirty-ton cargoes. Warehouse A was rated one of the finest warehouses in the area in 1989. Cleveland's lifting capacity was good. It made news in Detroit and Chicago when Ceres Terminals, Inc., used the Buckeye Booster for lifting heavy equipment out of the holds and onto the decks of transport vessels for later offloading at Detroit and Chicago. The overall Port tonnage and number of ships decreased, while average cargo per vessel rose. Movement of heavy equipment for carmakers continued.

Following Voinovich's advice for expanding involvement, in 1987 the Port hosted over 100,000 greater Clevelanders who visited ships and attended shore events. In September the Port welcomed approximately sixty members of Leadership Cleveland, many suburban mayors and city managers and county commissioners.

The Authority began planning for another set of visitors in 1991, when it would host the Annual Meeting and Convention of the American

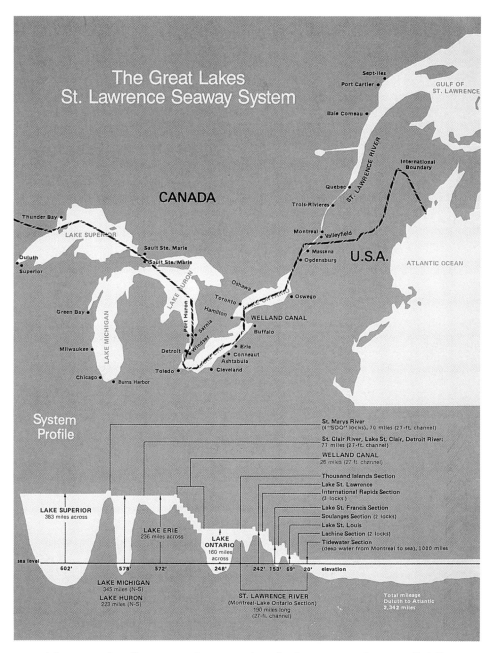

After more than four years of construction, the St. Lawrence Seaway officially opened to traffic on April 25, 1959. (Map courtesy of the St. Lawrence Seaway Development Corporation)

Queen Elizabeth II and President Dwight Eisenhower (right) dedicate the St. Lawrence Seaway at Montreal on June 26, 1959. (Cleveland Press Collection/CSU Archives)

Notice there are no wakes trailing these ships. In 1968, ten years after its opening, the Seaway is idled as 1,250 workers strike for higher pay. (Cleveland Press Collection/CSU Archives)

Work-a-day stevedore action shortly after the Seaway opening. (Cleveland Press Collection/CSU Archives)

The *Helen Miller* brought in a load of enormous Pielstick engines. The Buckeye Booster crane unloads them and gently tucks them onto a flatbed car.

Mayor Carl B. Stokes aggressively pressed for creation of a port authority. Here, he and Mrs. Stokes welcome one of the early foreign ship arrivals.

Harry Burmester, the first chairman of the Board of the Cleveland–Cuyahoga County Port Authority, is at right. With him is politically effective James Carney, dynamic member of the first Board.

The *Cadillac* is one of sixteen Maritime Class steamers built in the 1940s to carry iron ore for the war effort. She is shown here in 1975 being unloaded at the Lower Republic Steel Dock. She ran until 1980 for Cleveland Cliffs. (Courtesy of Alan W. Sweigert)

Icebound fleet in February 1981. (Cleveland Press Collection/CSU Archives)

Throughout the winter, export cargoes—here, steel coils—build up in Port warehouses ready to load when the ice breaks.

One interesting cargo, 250 tons of unpopped popcorn, here awaits loading onto the Yugoslav ship *Split*, bound for Rijeka, Yugoslavia.

Subject of years of acquisition negotiation by the Port was the Pennsylvania RR dock, pictured here in March 1964. (Cleveland Press Collection/CSU Archives)

A saltwater ship threads the needle at night—St. Lambert Lock opposite Montreal. (Cleveland Press Collection/CSU Archives)

Jay C. Ehle (at right), here with Mayor Michael White, was one of the few maritime-experienced Board members of the Port Authority. Ehle's long Board membership began in 1974 and ended on March 29, 1993. He served as chairman the last nine years. (Courtesy of Mort Tucker)

The Reverend Sterling E. Glover, current chairman of the Cleveland–Cuyahoga County Port Authority. (Courtesy of Mort Tucker)

Symbols of Cleveland—Port muscles and the landmark Terminal Tower.
(Cleveland Press Collection/CSU Archives)

Association of Port Authorities, Inc. (AAPA). In preparation for this, Admiral Fugaro joined the AAPA board of directors.

Finally in May 1988, Chairman Ehle announced that the lease with the city had been officially signed and was in effect. The terms included five years on Docks 28, 30, and 32; forty years on 24 and 26; and annual rent of $500,000. The Port immediately resumed its long-range planning and development operations.

Port management knew they would eventually be asked to vacate city property, and Board members needed an alternate plan that would enable them to effectively and quickly sustain shipping when notified to vacate specified docks. They needed to design facilities that would make efficient use of a smaller area.

In September 1989, they selected a consortium of Turner Construction, URS Consultants, and Polytech Inc. to draw preliminary plans for possible relocation west to the thirty-four-acre Dock 20 area near the Cuyahoga River, land purchased by the Port Authority in 1978.

In July the Authority was alarmed when the City Planning Commission approved Whiskey Island for recreational use, an action the Board emphatically opposed because it would destroy valuable deep-water docks. Cleveland's North Coast Harbor announced plans to build a Great Lakes Museum; the first half of which was to be at the southwest corner of the basin located between Municipal Stadium and East 9th Street.

On September 9, 1988, the North Coast Harbor officially opened with a three-day festival. Governor Celeste and Mayor Voinovich cut the ribbon spanning the harbor to dedicate Phase I of this "revitalization" program. Phase I included an eight-acre, man-made inner lake surrounded by a fifty-foot-wide promenade and an eight-acre landscaped park with a festival corner for events and concerts.

In 1988 vessels calling at the Port of Cleveland were registered to twenty different countries, manned mostly by Korean and Greek crews, and carried cargoes from Europe, the Far East, and South America. Because there were no American flag vessels in the Great Lakes, the Port of Cleveland was precluded from handling cargoes required to move strictly on American flag vessels.

The Polish MV *Ziemia Tarnowska* crashed into Dock 24 North while maneuvering to tie up, causing $175,000 damage.

In the last rush to finish work and exit the Seaway before the ice, 15,000 metric tons of steel were exported to India and heavy presses were handled for General Motors and Chrysler, but overall tonnage for 1988 was down 10 percent.

As Transall's lease for Dock 20 would expire in January of 1989, the dock returned to its status as a casual berth while the Port investigated other options. Casual status would generate income for the Port as well as additional employment both on and off the waterfront. However, to be ready for work, the dock needed emergency repairs. Filling, grading, rolling, and general road repairs were critical. The Port began this work.

First 1989 ship ceremonies welcomed the MV *La Richardais* from Antwerp. She unloaded steel and aluminum coils before continuing on to Toledo, Detroit, Chicago, and Duluth where a shipment of grain was loaded for the outbound trip.

Waterfront events during 1989 attracted thousands to the Port. In June almost 100,000 visitors toured the U.S. Coast Guard icebreaker *Mackinaw*. In August, people rushed to see the HMS *Bounty*, which had been used in the remake of the movie *Mutiny on the Bounty*.

Pursuing new business, Admiral Fugaro joined Governor Richard Celeste on the two-day Great Lakes governors diplomatic mission to Canada in May. Fugaro was also a member of the Governor's Ohio Lake Erie Shore Area Redevelopment Task Force, whose recommendations for the best and most effective uses of the Lake Erie shore area were incorporated into a twenty-year shore area redevelopment plan. In 1989 Fugaro also took part in a trade mission to Europe and North Africa.

In September, one of the Port of Cleveland's largest customers, Nebam, reported that Cleveland had the lowest damage claim rate of any port in the United States, yet Port insurance premiums ran over $88,000 in 1989!

Major Housekeeping

Warehouse A renovations completed, a portion of the warehouse became the long-awaited Foreign Trade Zone No. 40.

The management demolished an underutilized 7,500-square-foot structure at the south end of the warehouse on Dock 26 and filled in the truck dock in front of it. They removed old pavement and rail tracks, graded the area, installed a new drainage system, and repaved the entire dock.

Water level in Lake Erie was low, revealing several high spots. In October, several of these spots in the Port's slips were dredged to return them to a 27-foot depth. In some places dredging crews ran into wire cables thrown overboard by foreign ships, and these had to be picked up by special equipment before dredging could be completed.

Ship arrivals were down 12 percent, while overall tonnage was up 32 percent. Over 785,000 tons moved through the Port of Cleveland in

1989, its heaviest season since 1977. Steel slabs were again imported through the Port, and exporters of American steel and equipment shipped from Cleveland to India, Italy, Korea, and Japan.

United Engineering of Youngstown exported a complete, new steel mill to Taiwan. Experts felt the season would have topped 800,000 if the weather had held and the Canadian Coast Guard had not gone on strike.

The Port facility's value reached $517,789; to protect this investment, the Board hired Roy Knapp (formerly with Great Lakes Towing and the marine dock department of U.S. Steel) as its trade development manager. Lois M. Epstein handled public relations for six months; she was succeeded by Laura Vrabel, a dedicated and valuable asset to the Port.

Cleveland had a much better year than many other Great Lakes ports due to a steady flow of imports, good productivity of local industry, and the continued successful efforts of the Port Authority to provide an excellent facility and good service at a competitive price.

Remarkably, the Port achieved this with little help from its friends.

20

Changing of the Watch

A new mayor meant adjustments at the Port. When Governor George Voinovich left the Cleveland mayor's office in 1990 succeeded by young, ambitious, and Democratic Michael White, the chairman of the Port Authority was calmly aware that the recent changes in the city's perception of best use of its waterfront would now escalate sharply.

While Ehle and Glover continued in their posts for 1990, there were major Board changes. Vice Chairman Parker resigned to assume chairmanship of the Gateway project. Tom Wagner became vice chairman of the Port. Director Fred Crosby's term expired, and Mayor White appointed Ella Becton and Carla Tricarichi. Carl Glickman's term expired in April; he was replaced by Kenneth J. Fisher in June.

One Great Lakes editor, chronicling the Lakes for forty-three years, wrote in a profile of Ehle, "The chairman is the longest-serving director in the life of the Port Authority. He brought to the job a wide net of connections to industry, including unions. Since his arrival on the Port Authority Board, his net widened to governments, politicians, foundations, and civic improvement organizations. It gave him a unique perspective.

Ehle has seen enthusiastic concepts for alternative waterfront use rising on a fair wind later becalmed when the winds quit. Through it all he laconically held to the original

Seaway compass. Now, however, his wide-angle net is signaling a new movement accumulating broad support. The city seems to want the Port to face inland—parks, museums, restaurants, Rock Hall of Fame, and marinas. The chairman has always been a realist. He will make a seaport out of whatever space he has."

What Is a Port Worth to a City?

The Ohio Department of Transportation (ODOT) continued assistance as the Port completed a number of upgrading and relocation projects during 1990. One major undertaking was the rehabilitation of the dock fender system to protect both docks and ships, and ODOT grants provided much of the $166,000 cost.

Another ODOT grant covered 90 percent of the cost of an independent comprehensive economic impact study to assess the value of the Port to the community.

The results revealed that, in 1991, nearly 3,000 jobs, generating $30 million in personal income, were dependent on the Port of Cleveland. The $1.3 million in taxes received by the Port was shown to produce more than twice that amount annually in state and local taxes, as well as returning half a million dollars to the city in rent. The study concluded that the Port directly saved area industries

over $9 million in shipping costs each year and generated over $300 million in revenue for Port users.

Five years of continuous work by Representatives Mary Rose Oakar and Louis Stokes brought $750,000 for the Port's relocation planning. These funds were part of a $3-million reimbursement agreement with the U.S. Army Corps of Engineers and the Ohio Department of Natural Resources.

However, when estimated preliminary construction costs came in at over $50 million, the Port developed an alternative relocation plan that required vacating only Dock 32.

The Port presented the plan to all concerned interests in 1990, stressing the advantages of: saving the community $35 million; preserving irreplaceable docks to support area industries; and promoting public access to international shipping activities.

The plan met with enthusiastic support from city and county officials, area business interests, lakefront development, shipping interests, and other public organizations—a major coup.

In June, over two hundred influential guests arrived for the dedication of the newly activated Foreign Trade Zone No. 40. An aggressive marketing campaign promoted use of the zone by area importers and exporters. The Port staged a Foreign

Trade Zone seminar in cooperation with the Greater Cleveland Growth Association. Results were good, drawing interest from Picker International, Cleveland Pneumatic, Invacare, Agro-Tech, and twelve other shippers. Howard Broadbent proposed a plan to enlarge the location of the zone to include the entire Port area, which would allow activating other portions of the Port as a Foreign Trade Zone when advantageous.

Despite adverse economic conditions, the year's tonnage was second only to 1989's record levels. A late shipment of 17,000 tons of steel coils from LTV to Japan was the only steel export attributable to the dollar's strong hold against the Yen.

Concrete was in high demand for Cleveland's increased construction activity in 1990; Ontario Stone, which leased Dock 20 in June, helped supply those aggregates that helped raise the bulk cargo volume 210,000 tons above 1989 levels.

Six hundred port authority executives came to Cleveland for the AAPA 1991 convention hosted by the Port.

One of them, Dominic Taddeo, executive director for the Port of Montreal, commented, "my thanks . . . for a most informative, well organized and enjoyable 80th AAPA convention. The success of this event was clearly the product of a first class organization with top quality administrative support and I congratulate everyone for . . . an outstanding job." The Authority was particularly pleased that the convention was held at no expense to the taxpayers.

Coopers and Lybrand's annual audit showed that Port assets grew $1.1 million in 1991 with no deficiencies in the management of the Port's finances. The audit firm commented, "it is very rare for any public agency to receive such a report." (It is interesting to note that late in August 1992 the cost of shipping steel coils from Antwerp to Cleveland was $44.80 per ton. From that the Port received 60 cents!)

To sustain competitiveness, the Authority continued improving its facilities in 1991. It completed fendering and lighting upgrades and planned to place utility lines underground along Erieside. Engineering specifications were drawn up for a possible overhead crane in the Foreign Trade Zone. The Authority also planned to expand the Port's perimeter to include the entire Port property.

Visibility remained high due to the Port's new Dale Carnegie campaign, to its participation in groups such as the Technical Advisory Council and North Coast Harbor workshops, and to new leadership roles in the Greater Cleveland International Trade Alliance, the International Business Education Committee, the Cleveland World Trade Association, and the Advisory Board of Business and Industry 2000 (the joint venture of the I-X Center and the Greater Cleveland Growth Association). People came to the Port to tour the USS *Escotin* and the USCG *Mackinaw,* and staff members conducted Port tours and addressed community groups as they had in the previous year, when visitors to the Port toured the Coast Guard cutter *Escanaba,* the frigate USS *Fahrion,* and the tall ship HMS *Rose.* On August 2, 1990, there was an impressive double christening ceremony held by Interlake Steamship Company for two of its lakers, the SS *Kaye E. Barker* and the SS *Lee A. Tregurtha.*

To increase international trade through Cleveland, the Port participated in federally sponsored trade missions to Sweden, Poland, Belgium, the UK, and Spain. It also provided sponsorship for visiting trade delegations from the Soviet Union, Holland, Indonesia, Korea, Spain, Japan, and Lithuania. As a member of the Metropolitan Development Council, the Port participated in Mayor White's first Foreign Trade Mission to Toronto, Canada.

Work continued with the Regional Planning Commission of Greater Cleveland. Affirmative action was paramount; 42 percent of Port contracts went to minority-owned businesses. The Port worked throughout the year with the technical advisory council of the Cuyahoga County Planning Commission to create a solid waste management plan to export bulk waste such as cardboard, tire chips, and rags. It worked with the Green 21 Committee of the Cleveland Engineering Society on global recycling.

The year 1991 was a good one, with increased overall tonnage, higher steel exports, more applications for foreign trade subzones, higher bulk cargo across Dock 20, upgraded facilities, and continued good community relations.

In April 1992, new directors Dennis M. Lafferty and Stephen Rowan came aboard. By July, five of the nine directors were Mayor White appointees.

Upgrading and relocation projects continued with the help of state and federal grants. A major undertaking was the extension of Dock 24 by 75 feet to accommodate full Seaway-sized vessels. The Port completed Dock 26 lighting upgrades, extended the billet yard on Erieside, made substructure repairs on Docks 30 and 32, and repaved all truck and outdoor storage areas throughout the Port.

Admiral Fugaro and the ILA Great Lakes District president, John Baker, joined a foreign trade mission sponsored by the Seaway Development Corporation. They visited Finland, Estonia, Russia, Czechoslovakia, Austria, and Hungary to promote direct transportation of goods to and from the Great Lakes region.

Surprise

There was a disappointing first for the Port Authority in 1992 with the defeat of the renewal levy by less than 1 percent of the total vote. The loss was attributed to a record turnout (with many first-time voters unaware of the importance of the Port), baffling ballot language, a small levy promotion budget, and complacency—"The Port levies always pass. Why worry?"

It is interesting to note that this Port, and most ports, have been regular targets for media criticism. Yet Cleveland media seldom noted the conflict-filled environment in which the Port managers somehow built a very successful operation. None noted how they had built the Port's asset value.

The Port intensified community relations in preparation for the levy's reappearance on the November 1993 ballot with a promotional videotape distributed widely around the county. It invited public tours and promoted visits to the USS *Samuel Eliot Morison* and the USCG *Mackinaw*. The Port participated in the Coasts Week Festival, the Fire Engine Buffs Convention on July 11, off-shore power boat races on July 17, and annual Port Night at Cleveland Stadium.

Any port can turn in splendid dock performance day-in, day-out unnoticed. Broad media coverage often comes from some trivial actions, such as when the Cleveland Port lent a hand to help a group of Russian sailors return *Aira,* their handmade 37-foot sloop, to their hometown of Volvograd. The sloop was hoisted from the water at the Port and placed on jacks, crated for shipment, and put on a Russian liner. As the Russians had no resources, it took combined efforts of the Port Authority, the ILA, and Ceres Terminals to accomplish this.

On May 17 there were five ships docked in the Port, including the specially built vessel, MV *Trans Scandic.* This ship had managed a cargo of asphalt with a crew of only ten! Another Russian ship would carry 572 tons of fumigated oak and walnut logs to Germany.

Another first—the Russian MV *Kapitan Radionov* discharged 7,500 tons of coal tar from the Ukraine directly to barges for transfer up the Cuyahoga.

S. Clifford, of the Regional Industry Center, questioned the Board about Consolidated Rail Corporation's (CRC) announcement that they would abandon the rail system on Whiskey Island. Specifically, Clifford asked the Port Authority to tell CRC to defer dismantling the Hulett unloaders pending an indepth financial analysis. The chairman explained that the Port could not dictate policy to private corporations.

Tax receipts in 1992 accounted for 40 percent of the Port's income, compared to 51 percent in 1988. This was a giant step toward the Port's goal of operating only on its own income.

As the year ended, the essence and philosophy of the Port was about to change drastically from that of the past twenty-four years. For example, a change had been made in the Port development plan to enable the Rock and Roll Hall of Fame and Museum construction to proceed as a recreational project. The Hall was to be largely financed and controlled by the Port, which would require additional staff and organization. The Great Lakes Science Museum was sure of a place.

Under the provisions of the Ohio Revised Code, the Port had extensive economic development powers; and under its mandate to create and preserve jobs, the Port began using this power to meet the growing needs of its community beyond shipping.

Control of Dock 12 was transferred from the Port to the city. Exploration was in progress for locating the new aquarium. Should it be built from Dock 28 to 32 and/or at Dock 20? The Port was working hard to explain the economies of going to Dock 20 (also the first choice of the aquarium board).

As a first step, the Authority formed an Economic Development Division. It passed a formal resolution that authorized the Port to participate in development of a plan to acquire, finance, construct, and equip an educational and cultural facility (the Rock and Roll Hall of Fame and Museum) and appointed a financial team.

In 1993, Chairman Ehle submitted a new slate of officers: Sterling Glover, chairman and CEO; Renold Thompson, vice chairman; Howard Broadbent, secretary.

Jay C. Ehle was invited to be reappointed, but he resigned. He had been on the Board since 1974 and had served as chairman since 1984. Ehle's leadership had successfully guided the Port through torrents of recession and politics. A maritime man, he faced seaward on the job.

Sterling Glover's job might be to face inland.

21

Quo Vadis?

Athens on Lake Erie
"If We Build It, They Will Come"

Ports are gateways to their cities' commerce and as well as to the character of the regions. Cleveland's working docks speak of the city's metallurgical muscle. However, today the lakefront is projecting the other powerful face of the Western Reserve—its historic, cultural side. The city began at the Port, then moved inland; now it returns to the Port.

At water's edge will rise a low-silhouette skyline, anchored by three world-class museums. Around these will rise satellites.

Music at the Port

On September 4, 1995, the Rock and Roll Hall of Fame and Museum opened its glamorous glass front amid fanfare and to an excited international throng.

If one thought the Rock Hall's music might have a provincial following, a different impression comes from the director, a relaxed, confident museum veteran with a trim graying beard. Dennis Barrie paints a picture of the Rock Hall's future as an international center. He speaks of international alliances by the score and international visitors by the thousands.

Paradoxically, the ultramodern structure on the lakefront captures the eye in the same way that the nearby antique Huletts stopped traffic.

Since 1986, the Rock and Roll Hall of Fame has inducted over 120 performers, nonperformers, and early influencers of this dominant and enduring music. With the June 7, 1993, groundbreaking, Cleveland officially became home to the Museum. By September 1995, $80 million had been invested in the 150,000-square-foot museum.

Dennis Barrie says that interior exhibits have "attitude, openness, and public accessibility. We are using a lot more film, a lot more technology . . . and performers are inundating us with so much memorabilia that many exhibits will rotate quarterly."

The facility also includes comprehensive archives and a library; working studio for radio and television broadcast; simulated production studios, sound booths, and presentation areas for visitor use; an outdoor arena for concerts; and an indoor theater with 125 seats for performances.

The project continues to draw a wealth of international talent and attention to Cleveland, beginning with Dennis Barrie. While he was director of the Contemporary Arts Center in Cincinnati from 1983–92, its membership increased from 400 to 3,500; its budget from $400,000 to $1.4 million; annual attendance from 20,000 to 100,000; and endowment from zero to nearly $1 million. After his arrival in Cleveland, the Rock Hall moved from dream to reality, and his enthusiasm for the Cleveland lakefront development is contagious.

I. M. Pei, internationally acclaimed architect, designed the building to mirror the movement, energy, and action of the music itself. Some of his other recent work includes the East Building of the National Gallery of Art in Washington, the John F. Kennedy Library in Boston, the Museum of Modern Art in Athens, and the Grand Louvre in Paris.

Projecting a relaxed, matter-of-fact conviction, Barrie predicts, "I think [the museums] will generate a sort of people-oriented redevelopment that I don't think we can even fathom right now."

Great Waters of the World

When Bruce V. Mavec, chairman of the Great Waters of the World, the aquarium planned for the lakefront, says "if we build it, they will come," he's referring to the million visitors a year drawn to what is planned as the nation's greatest aquarium.

Imagine walking along the bottom of Lake Erie in street clothes, with no scuba gear, surrounded on all sides by muskies, perch, pike, and shipwrecks. How could that be done?

Imagine, again without diving equipment, traveling vertically and horizontally under the ocean along the Great Barrier Reef off Australia, the spectacular 200-mile live coral reef with its brilliant kaleidoscope of fishes. How could this be done?

Imagine being surrounded on four sides by the underwater life of the world's greatest river system, the Nile. How could that be arranged?

Mavec is accustomed to arranging the difficult. He built a lot of Greater Cleveland.

An erudite developer with a practical mastery of both the civic and political landscape, Mavec exercises a pleasant but powerful negotiating skill that moves projects.

In the case of walking the bottom of Lake Erie surrounded on all sides by fish, it will be done with acrylic. We will be walking, perfectly dry, through a 200-foot acrylic tunnel in a million-gallon tank. As for viewing all levels of the Great Barrier Reef, we'll be riding a platform up three stories of a 140,000 gallon transparent tank. As for the Nile, viewers will be surrounded on four sides by a huge tank.

Bruce Mavec is known to his friends as a global thinker, and he surrounds himself with like thinkers. Hence, the name of the future aquarium is Great Waters of the World.

Their idea is not merely to show us a lot of fancy fish. Worldly enough to understand the importance of some show business packaging, the big deception they plan here is to surreptitiously show us our responsibility in the care and handling of our world, which is three-quarters aquatic. They will show our affect upon the global environment: our actions in one location project by waters to environments thousands of

miles downstream, affecting millions of people and animals, including the unborn.

For school students, that view will be formalized and structured. But the perpetrators of this grand deception are informed enough to know that adults won't stand still for lectures or tours. Therefore, the exhibit designers' intense challenge is to make the exhibits speak for themselves. Hence, the huge Nile River Basin presentations show the affect on 38 million people in fourteen African nations.

There will be a glass-domed Sudd Swamp exhibit of the fish, birds, and reptiles in the world's most hostile environment.

The major Antarctica exhibit will show a primal environment not yet trampled by humankind.

On the scholarly side again, the aquarium intends to be a dissemination center for the good and extensive research now coming out of the universities.

The planners are aware of what aquariums have done for other regions. The National Aquarium in Baltimore is the largest public draw in Maryland. New England Aquarium on Boston's once-hard-boiled waterfront led to development of grand hotels, housing, and offices. The same results occurred in Monterey Bay, California, and in New Orleans.

In Cleveland, Mavec, his staff, and some very down-to-earth business people on the board are sure that, "If we build it, they will come."

The Science Adventure

Frederick C. Crawford, Cleveland's dean of industrial technology, has said, "The technological adventure of the next decade will dwarf the last fifty."

Cleveland needs to be ready for that trip.

Structurally dominating this new lakefront Athens will be the elegant Great Lakes Science Center, now rising.

Richard Coyne is brisk, intense, and all business. A veteran museum executive, he is aware of all the great science museums in the world. Dedicated to making this the world's best, he is necessarily always in a hurry.

The great themes will be the interlocking of science, technology, and environment, coming alive on three floors of interconnecting exhibit areas. A 320-seat Omnimax Theater will dramatize science on the world's largest screen and projection system.

Hands-on exhibits will dominate. By touch and manipulation, the visitor will get the thrill of understanding. What once seemed arcane abstractions suddenly will become— "A-hah!"—clear.

The Science Center's Environmental Exhibition area will present concepts for solving the great dilemma of how to sustain scientific advances for man without increasing pressure on the environment. Exhibits on this theme will explore such concerns as acid rain, bioaccumulation, ozone depletion, and global warming. The environmental area will present major exploration of the vast Great Lakes ecosystem, offering solutions for preservation.

Three technology galleries will focus strongly on those industries that built northern Ohio's economy. Some other exhibits will be future-looking and include such subjects as biomedical progress, polymer science, artificial intelligence, and virtual reality.

There will be dramatic demonstrations of five basic scientific inquiries—light optics, sound and resonance, motion and mechanics, electricity and magnetism, and weather phenomena—to add to our understanding natural laws and how the world works.

The Omnimax Theater, with its dramatic way of putting the viewer in the middle of the action, with image on all sides and above and below, will place visitors inside glaciers, rain forests, and tornadoes.

A Math-Science Resource Center will offer a library of computer programs and teacher training materials.

Technical literacy at all levels is fast becoming a make-or-break imperative for a modern society. One might say it always has been. However, the present accelerated pace (in which the microchip doubles in power every eighteen months) is not matched by present educational resources. The Science Center expects to alleviate, at least regionally, the crisis in science education and to become a force for inspiring scientific understanding and enthusiasm.

The Big Semicircle

The full rebirth of the region comes from the aerial view. Just to the west of this new Port lakefront is a new marina. Along a half-mile inland stretch astride the river thrives a new mile-long entertainment area, the Flats, which light up at night. Atop the escarpment is Public Square, renewed with the Society and BP towers and The Avenue. Only a short throw south is the nation's newest sports/entertainment complex, Jacobs Field and Gund Arena. Sixteen blocks east is the revitalized Playhouse Square's three theaters restored to their 1930s gold-leaf grandeur. Add to that the renowned square-mile cluster of eighty-five cultural institutions—museums, a university, and hospitals—known as University Circle. Though launched in the 1800s by the same men who built and used the Port, the Circle today bristles with new construction. Looping north from the center, three miles of Cultural Gardens follow Martin Luther King Boulevard back to the lake.

From the Port to the Gardens, all these developments form a huge semicircular renaissance.

While professional directors, recruited from the nation's best, are in charge of building the new lakefront skyline, the creative start-up force was the same type of Cleveland citizen leadership that built the institutions of University Circle and the Port.

When Captain Ramagathan of the India vessel *Punica* brings her back to the Port in 1996, he will see a new Port skyline.

The author sends his best wishes to Chairman Sterling Glover and the Board and the staff.

Index

Cleveland's Harbor
was composed in 10½/13 Minion on a Power Macintosh 7100/80
by The Kent State University Press;
imaged to film and printed by sheet-fed offset
on Glatfelter 50-pound Supple Opaque Natural stock
(an acid-free recycled paper),
with halftones printed on 70-pound enamel stock,
notch bound over binder's boards in Arrestox B-grade cloth,
and wrapped with dustjackets printed in two colors
on 100-pound enamel stock
finished with matte film lamination
by Thomson-Shore, Inc.;
designed by Will Underwood;
and published by

THE KENT STATE UNIVERSITY PRESS
Kent, Ohio 44242